The Missing Detective

David Blanco Laserna

The Missing Detective

5C13NC3 COD3

ANAYA ENGLISH

1st edition: may 2014

Juan Ignacio Luca de Tena, 15. 28027 Madrid
www.anayainfantilyjuvenil.com
e-mail: anayainfantilyjuvenil@anaya.es

ISBN: 978-84-678-6141-9
Depósito legal: M-6789-2014
Printed in Spain

Contents

Appendix

To Julita and Tito,
for their terrace, their rocking chair
and their mystery novels.

CHAPTER ONE

A blank mind

It was like waking up from a profound dream, but... it wasn't. He immediately knew there was something wrong. He wasn't wearing his pyjamas or lying in bed. His only pillow was a strong feeling of cold that was so intense that it had left his cheek numb. When he opened his eyes, he found himself lying face down on the snow. He looked around. The wind was shaking a lamp that was hanging from a hook, over his head. The flashes of light were lighting the wooden sign of a wine warehouse, some wine barrels, the trap door to a coal bunker. The bricks on the walls formed the drawing in perspective of a dark alley. From the end of it he could hear the sounds of the city, muffled by the distance: the voices of street vendors, the paperboys delivering the morning newspapers, the hooves of horses on the paving...

"What has happened to me?" he asked himself, "how did I get here?"

There was a little frost on his eyelids. The hand he put on the floor to push himself up was purplish and he could hardly move his swollen fingers. He guessed that he must have spent about an hour there, lying unconscious on the floor. As he tried to stand up, he felt a growing nausea. Some kind of irresistible force was pulling him back down on the floor, and he had to hold onto a post so as not to fall over.

What were those dark shadows he could see in the snow? He half-closed his eyes to focus them better. Had he dropped a handkerchief on the floor? Maybe a watch? It took him half a minute to realise they were bloodstains. He instinctively touched his neck, were there was a tickling, warm and wet feeling. When he looked at his hand, he found it covered in blood. He slid his fingers upwards, little by little, from the back of his neck and when he touched the crown of his head he felt an intense pain that made him shout.

He was short of breath. "What has happened to me?" He tried to remember, but his mind was as blank as the snow he was stepping on. Panic took over him. "Who am I?" How could he be asking himself that question? And what was even more terrifying: *Why wasn't he able to answer it?* In the fog that surrounded his thoughts he couldn't find a name or a familiar face. He couldn't remember his home, his age or even what he looked like. He spent many minutes with an open mouth. "I don't know who I am, I don't know who I am, *I don't know who I am*". His heart was beating so hard that he could feel his heartbeats in his temples, in his ears and in the veins of his fingers.

He felt like crying. He took a deep breath. What could he do? Who could he ask to help him? He stared at the floor as he tried to calm down. Two trails of footprints surrounded the hole that his body had left in the snow. They had been made by two different pairs of shoes. He noticed that the footprints of one of the trails were exactly the same size as the worn out soles of his boots. They were his own footprints. The others were footprints of a more elegant type of shoe, with a square toe box. They belonged to someone else. Before becoming unconscious he had been having a conversation with someone. The footprints of the stranger came from the opening to the alley, stopped right at the point where he had fallen and then turned back to go away. The distance between the footprints was shorter on their way to where he was than on their way back. When someone runs, the distance between their footsteps becomes bigger: the stranger had walked up to him at a relaxed pace and had then left in a hurry. Why? He looked at his bloodstained hand. The stranger had hit him by surprise from behind. He may have tried to kill him. But again, he asked himself the same question: Why?

It was starting to snow again, not very heavily yet, but in an hour's time another thick layer of snow would cover the footprints. He didn't have the time to follow both trails. Which one should he follow? His own footprints might lead him home. His attacker's might expose him to dangers that he wasn't even able to imagine. He only hesitated for an instant. The rage and indignation he was feeling led him to trying to catch the mysterious who had run away after leaving him, with his bloodstained head, in a miserable alley.

He slipped on the snow, on his way out, while he pressed his fist against his wound to stop it bleeding. As soon as he got to Dorset Street, he had to face many problems. He didn't have a hat to cover his wounded head. Everyone he crossed in the street, whether they were tall or short, handsome or ugly, fat or thin, they all looked away and hastened their pace. “I must look terrible”, he moaned to himself. He saw his own reflection on the shop window of a tea and coffee shop. He was scared by his cadaveric expression and immediately looked away. But the look was long enough to know he was young. He guessed he must be about fifteen years old.

His main concerns now was to try not to faint and to try not to lose the track of his own footprints. He noticed that his own walking was leaving footprints of the same depth as the stranger's. Therefore, the person who had attacked him weighed more or less the same as him. Otherwise, his footprints would have been deeper or shallower. He didn't know for how long he had been walking, always looking for his square toe-box footprints in the snow, shivering, with his teeth clicking together until he reached a tall iron gate, and he couldn't walk any further.

He was in an affluent neighbourhood, with broad and well-kept streets. Everywhere he looked he could see a display of majestic mansions of every architectural styles. Between the bars of the gate in front of him there was a puzzling coat of arms. Instead of castles or rampant lions, it had the picture of a prism and a test tube over a field of stars. At the top of the coat of arms there were three big golden capital letters: GKC. He tried pushing the gate, without much hope. To his surprise, it opened with a creak, which scared away a flock of sleepy sparrows. On the other side there was a big lawn esplanade. There were big chestnut trees covered in snow on each side of a winding gravel path that went uphill, leading to an impressive house. Its roof was composed of tens of tiny little roofs, all of them forming what looked like an army of chimneys. Their plumes of smoke got together into an ashy cloud that hung over the house. Someone had cleared the snow from the path with a shovel, erasing the footprints that he had been following.

While he examined the façade, the young man took air and wondered what the hell he was doing there. An inner voice warned him that putting his head in the lion's mouth. What if his attacker was precisely the owner of that residence? He was still in time to escape from danger. To tell the truth he wasn't in the right conditions to fight even a tiny beetle. He could hardly stand on his feet. The sensation of fear made him feel even colder and he wanted to turn back.

Dickson Carr, the butler of the mansion, heard the doorbell ring while he was polishing a pair of lobster tongs. He checked the pendulum clock in the living room. It was quarter to twelve. He frowned. It certainly was an unexpected visit. He dropped the tongs and the cloth. On his way to the entrance door, he rearranged his uniform and combed his eyebrows with a finger. Dickson received newcomers with a neutral and polite expression that could later evolve quickly into strong rejection or open hospitality.

'Good afternoon,' he said, as he opened the door. 'How can I help you?'

Dickson had asked this question in an automatic way, with his eyes half-open, while his head was still thinking about the scratches that he had found on some of the tongs.

'I'm looking for...' As the stranger spoke, the butler opened his eyes progressively until they were wide open. In front of him there was a trembling young man with a livid and blood-stained face. The boy couldn't finish the explanation of what he was looking for. He collapsed at his feet like a card castle.

Dickson had served in an infantry regiment during the Indian Mutiny, so he wasn't impressed by the sight of blood. As efficiently as he managed every domestic problem, he pulled the young man up and took him through the air to the nearest room, the billiards room, where he put him on a divan. He asked Miss Marsh to bring some bandage and a washbasin with hot water and soap. After stopping the bleeding, cleaning the wound and calling a doctor, he rearranged his uniform, combed his eyebrows and went to the library to inform Mr Crispin that a little mishap was going to alter the activities they had programmed for the afternoon.

* * *

Before the young man could regain consciousness for a second time, he had to find his way through a foggy dream. He saw himself in a forest, in front of an old witch doctor with ram legs. It was snowing and the witch doctor had cast a spell for his hair to fall at the same pace as the snowflakes. In the blink of an eye, the old man disappeared, and reappeared again, just a few centimetres away from his face. He stretched his knotty and crooked fingers, and held his head with them. He felt a strong pain in the back of his neck. The young man moved violently to try to shake the old man off him, but a pair of very firm hands were holding him.

'He's woken up.'

'I can see that. Stay still! Stay still, kid! *If you don't, I'm going to cut you…* Calm down. We're trying to cure you.'

He could recognise the smell of iodine. A pair of hands with very firm fingers were manipulating his head. The back of his neck felt as cold as ice. They had shaved it. In the position that he was in, with his cranium immobilised, he had an oblique perspective of the room, well lit by a gas lamp that was hanging from the ceiling. He noticed there was a wash-basin on a table, with a sponge sticking out of it. Next to it there was a reel of surgical thread. They were sowing up his wound. A smiley face with a big curly moustache that looked like the handles of a bicycle entered his visual field.

'I am doctor Nathan Thorndyke,' the owner of the moustache introduced himself. 'I have shaved part of your head to clean your wound, disinfect it and stitch it up. I've just given you the last stitches and now I'm going to bandage your head.'

His profound voice combined the authority and the automatic cordiality that doctors usually have. The young man let the doctor do what he had to do. He was lying on a canopy bed, with his legs covered with a pile of blankets.

The height of the mattress and the scent of the sheets made him realise he wasn't at home. It was a puzzling feeling of certainty, because he didn't even have the remotest idea of what his house was like. He then remembered his horrendous awakening in the alley, the anguish of not knowing who he was. He experienced a sudden glimmer of hope. He was remembering! If his memory had been able to go back to the moment of the accident, could it go even further back in the past?

'Are you all right?'

He turned his neck slowly and saw a second individual, an old man who was holding a kerosene lamp over his head to illumine the bandaging operation, which he was watching with a critical attitude.

'I've got a terrible headache,' he admitted while he clenched his teeth.

'That's normal,' doctor Thorndyke said, reassuringly.

'Really?'

'It's normal when someone has cracked your head open. But don't worry, nothing has come out of it. What's your name, young man?'

He instinctively tried to answer. However, something stopped him from doing so. It was on the tip of his tongue, but it wouldn't come out. Did his name begin with J? With H? With S? Joseph? Bell? Fletcher? The answer couldn't have been erased from his memory, even if it insisted on remaining out of his reach. His memories had sunk like a galleon does under the weight of its treasures. And they refused to come back afloat. After making the effort for one minute, he gave up.

'I don't know.'

'That's all right.' The old man tried to calm him down with an encouraging smile. 'My name's Gideon Keith Crispin. I'm the owner of this house. Do you remember what happened to you?'

'No, I can't remember that either.'

'Do you know where you are?' Doctor Thorndyke took over, while he delicately adjusted the last end of the bandage. 'What city?'

'In York?'

'No, you are in London. In one of the most affluent neighbourhoods, by the way.' Thorndyke looked at Gideon mockingly. 'Do you know the address of anyone in your family? Do you know what your father does for a living?'

The young man made an even bigger effort than before to remember. Finally, he dropped his head on the pillow, with his forehead full of sweat.

'No, I don't.'

'What's my name?' the doctor asked.

'Doctor Thorndyke. And this gentleman is Mr Gideon Keith Crispin.'

The doctor smiled, pleased with the answer.

'We aren't doing so badly. Can you follow the movements of my finger? Very good. Now try to touch your left cheek with your right hand. That's it. What's our Serene Highness's name?'

'Victoria.'

'Well, don't worry. You're suffering from retrograde posttraumatic amnesia. You will remember everything that happens to you from now onwards. If you're interested in the part of your history that happened before, the normal thing would be for you to start to progressively recover your memory in the next few hours. Although it could take weeks.'

The young man bit his lips:

'And could it be forever?'

Thorndyke started to pick up the reel of thread, a surgical needle and the bottle of iodine.

'We doctors usually base ourselves on probability, and the most probable thing is that you will recover your memory in a few hours' time.'

'Can I ask you another question?'

'We've asked you many,' Thorndyke smiled, pinching his moustache. 'It seems fair to me. Go ahead.'

'After having examined the wound, how do you think it was made?'

The doctor thought about the question for a few seconds.

'I think I know where you're heading. You want to know if it happened by accident. If, for instance, a roof tile fell on you or if you lost your balance and hit yourself against something on the floor,' he denied it by shaking his head with a grave expression. 'I would say someone hit you from behind, from top to bottom, heavily, but with a not very heavy object. Not very sharp either. When I cleaned your wound I found wooden splinters... I would bet it was a club or a stake.'

The doctor closed his briefcase and went to pick up his coat, which he had left on the back of an armchair.

'Well, it's been a pleasure. Good luck with your memory... I hope you like your memories when they come back.'

He slightly bowed his head as a way to say goodbye. Gideon went with the doctor to the corridor, softly closing the door behind them. On the bedside table there was a glass of water. The young man drank it at once, jumped out of bed and walked on his tiptoes to the door. He put the brim of the glass on the wooden plank, and put his ear on the base of the glass. On the other side, Mr Crispin and doctor Thorndyke were whispering, but the surface of the glass could pick up their words and amplified them to make them clear enough.

'And what are the... formalities of this case?'

'As soon as he gets out of here I need to talk to the sergeant on duty and write a report.'

'And then...'

'They will call him to take a statement from him...'

'Which, given the circumstances, will not be very long.'

'Well, no, it doesn't look as if he has a lot to say. The normal thing would be that while they carry out an investigation they kept him under house arrest, but, as he isn't able to say what his home address is, he will probably end up in a prison cell.'

'What a pity, Thorndyke, what a pity. Just at Christmas time. And you say that the best thing to do...'

'...in these cases is to let him rest as much as he can. The less anxiety he experiences, the better.'

'The prison doesn't seem a very relaxing kind of place.'

The doctor shrugged his shoulders.

'I would prefer a health resort, but the precepts of medicine are very different from those of the law.'

Mr Crispin took a moment for some thoughtful silence.

'He may be in danger too. If they have attacked him once, they could do it again... He's defenceless without his memory,' he coughed before continuing. 'And what if we don't tell the authorities about it and let him stay here for a few days? Until he is able to manage on his own.'

The doctor shrugged his shoulders.

'That's a very kind thing for you to do, providing that you...'

'You have not come here today. I opened the door to him, I cleaned his wound, I bandaged him, and on my own responsibility I let him stay.'

Nathan Thorndyke picked up his hat from a hanger on the wall and put it on with an astute expression.

'I see that we understand each other well. And as I haven't been here, I'd better leave as soon as possible.'

Mr Crispin shook his hand.

'Thank you, Thorndyke.'

'You're welcome, Gideon. We've already done our good deed of the year. Merry Christmas!'

The young man returned to his bed, walking unsteadily. A few seconds after, Mr Crispin opened the door carefully. The light that came in from the corridor let him see the peculiar looks that his host had. Mr Gideon Keith Crispin was so bony and small that he looked like a ventriloquist puppet that someone had taken out from a drawer. His prominent eye sockets and cheeks gave him a chimpanzee-like air, which was further accentuated by his stooping back, his long little arms and his short height. He protected his bald head with a red velvet cap, from which there were some white, long and thin hairs coming out, which flew about him whenever he moved. He was wearing a pair of red checked trousers and an extravagant mustard coloured waistcoat, and was holding a walking stick.

'Do you remember me?' he asked mockingly.

The young man nodded. Gideon rolled up his trousers and sat down on a corner of the bed. The mattress gave very little under his weight.

'I wanted to tell you that I've got a proposal for you. Let's see what you think. You can stay in my home for as long as you need, until your wound is healed, or you recover your memory or until you feel strong enough to face the world again. Without any time limitations, without any pressures. If you want to leave tomorrow, well, you can leave tomorrow. If you prefer to wait for a month, well, you wait for a month.'

The young man got a lump in his throat. After all the anguish and abandonment he had felt in the last few hours, that old man's kindness disarmed him completely. He felt a strong desire to embrace him, but in the 19th century, men simply didn't embrace each other. To express their affection, they patted each other on the back. But this was

something that the young man didn't feel strong enough to do, and that Mr Crispin probably wouldn't resist.

'Thank you,' he said with a trembling voice.

'There's no need to say that,' Mr Crispin nodded with satisfaction. 'As soon as I leave the room I'll talk to everyone so that when you get up you won't have to give explanations to everyone. They are very nice people, you'll see. There are usually very few of us here: Mr Dickson, the butler; Mrs Marsh, the maid, and Mrs Sayers, the cook. However, you have come to visit us at a special time and we have four guests.'

'Members of your family who have come over to spend Christmas with you?'

'No, not at all. I am the last Crispin. A very old mummy without any descendants. The only family I have left is two aunts, two old bags, even older than me, who live in Cornwall.' Gideon opened his eyes very widely as if everything in this world caused him great surprise. 'I'm also what newspapers call an eccentric millionaire. Which means I inherited a fortune and I don't spend it the way most journalists would want me to.'

The young man smiled.

'And what do you spend it on?'

'I like science, you see?' Mr Crispin lowered his voice, as if this were an embarrassing confession. 'When I was your age I wanted to be a chemist, an astronomer, a mathematician, all at the same time, but I haven't been able to finish any degree course. I'm terrible at studying! I dreamt of discovering a planet, or a new kind of beetle or of proving the theorem of Crispin... Well, in the end I managed to do these things, but in my own way. I fund universities, museums, laboratories... If you look for my name in a scientific book, you will find it at the beginning, on the acknowledgements page. My latest initiative has been to set up a competition for young investigators. I've invited the four finalists to stay here at my home for three weeks. I've organised some meetings with great scientists. They have met Charles Darwin and James Clerk Maxwell. They have been able to do some experimenting in my laboratory and spend the night in my astronomical observatory. Tomorrow we will announce the name of the winner, who will receive a grant of fifty pounds.

Gideon noticed the signs of fatigue on the young man's face, who was making a titanic effort not to fall asleep.

'I'm sorry, there's only one thing that I like more than science: talking all the time.'

He got up from the bed and turned off the gas tap. The only source of light left was the kerosene lamp he was holding.

'One last thing: until you remember your real name, we'll have to call you some way.' After thinking for a few seconds, he could see in his eyes a sparkle of sudden inspiration. 'How about "Nemo"?'

'Nemo? Like the captain from *Twenty Thousand Leagues Under the Sea*?'

'That's right! So you have read the book.'

'So it seems,' the young man answered, a little perplexed.

'Jules Verne is my favourite author. *Nemo* means "Nobody". He was an Indian prince and that bandage that our friend Thorndyke has put around your head makes look like a true maharaja. It's perfect.'

The young man didn't feel like arguing. Besides, he couldn't deny that it seemed a practical idea.

'All right. Until I can find a better alternative, my name will be Nemo.'

'All right then, young Nemo. Consider yourself at home. When you wake up, you will have Mrs Sayers's plum cake waiting for you. Even if you can't remember how the others tasted, you can take my word on this: it will be the most exquisite one you will have ever tried.'

Nemo nodded and, on board of his own personal *Nautilus*, he sank into a profound sleep.

CHAPTER TWO

On guard

He was awaken by an unpleasant buzz in his ears. His stitches were stinging under the bandage and his mind was still drifting, floating on a sea of pain. However, a powerful spring, the strength of his personality, was moving him to get out of bed and become active.

He got up very slowly and got dressed with the clothes that he found folded on a stool, at the foot of the bed. While he did it, he noticed there was a big mirror next to the corner of the window. He felt a profound anxiety. What could his face look like? The shop window of the tea and coffee shop had left too vague an impression on him. He approached the mirror very slowly, divided between the pressing need to know and an absurd dread of finding a deformed face. His looks provoked on him the same impression as any stranger would. From his reflection there was a young man with piercing eyes, hawk nose and square chin, staring at him. He was neither very tall nor very short, although the fact that he was slim, made him look a little taller. He could be about fifteen or sixteen years old. He was wearing casual clothes. His long hair, green jacket with elbow patches and red scarf, gave him a bohemian appearance. His clothing was certainly not that of a labourer, or a servant, or a shop-assistant. He didn't look like a businessman, a nobleman or a land owner either. An Art student maybe? He didn't know if he liked his face. In fact he seemed to notice an air of arrogance in his face that he disliked a little.

He dug into his jacket pockets and extended their contents on the bedspread: a pocket watch and two small paper parcels. On the cover of the watch he noticed there were two carved letters: S.H. Could they be the initials of his name? Sean Hastings? Stanley Hodgson? Sheridan Hawking? He untied the cord of the parcels. The first one had a wad of banknotes in it. He counted them carefully. There were a hundred pounds, a considerable amount of money. Could they be his savings? He anxiously scratched his neck, right below the bandage. Could it be stolen money? The second parcel contained even more puzzling things: three bronze coloured stones. There was something exotic in them, which made him think they came from another planet. They were hard and were covered with a rough crust of tiny crystals.

His coat was hanging from the coat hook. He dug into its pockets and took from them a ball of clay, about the size of an olive. He made it roll on the palm of his hand. He must have squashed it with his body when he had fallen in the alley. There was only a little portion of it that hadn't been squashed, where three vertices of a polyhedron could be seen.

A hundred pounds, a pocket watch with two initials carved on it, three stones and a ball of clay… Three objects were the elements of a hieroglyphic that he couldn't decipher. The money seemed very solid indication that he was involved in some shady business. He shrugged his shoulders. The hit on his head had erased every worry about the past, except for one: who had attacked him and why? The only clue he had were the footprints of some shoes. To be on the safe side, he hid the money and the stones at the bottom of a decorative urn, on the mantelpiece of the fireplace.

The hours he had spent sleeping, instead of relieving his dizziness, had made it even worse. When he came out of the room, he tried to orientate himself. He was on the second floor of the mansion, in a corridor that went around the stairwell. He checked what time it was with a clock on the table: it was half past five. By the position of the sun he deduced that the wall at the end was the wall of the entrance façade. He walked with a limp.

To his left, over the lintel of a glass door, there was a sign hanging with the word *laboratory*. On the other side of the frosted glass, the rows of workbenches could be vaguely seen. Further along the corridor, two metres after the door, there was a voice escaping from the cracks in the last door, opposite the staircase. Although it sounded muffled, it did transmit its sense of impatience. Nemo couldn't help pressing his ear to the door.

'Come on, Poe. Come on! We haven't got all afternoon… Come right away! Don't be stubborn. You can tell we are Virginians, can't you? All right! Do you want to act the fool? Well, now you're grounded without dinner!'

A series of bangs made the wall tremble, and some footsteps could be heard coming nearer. Nemo rushed down the stairs, with his head turned, staring over his shoulder at the door, which didn't open. It seemed clear that in Gideon K. Crispin's mansion, not everyone was as kind as its owner. Could that mysterious voice belong to his attacker?

As he turned his head to look forward, Nemo was about to crash agains a gigantic Christmas tree. Its fairy lights dazzled him. It was the first time he saw a Christmas tree with electric fairy lights. Although he couldn't remember it, until then he had only known the traditional lighting with candles. The fir tree was so big that to adorn it they had used a sea of silver tinsel, little paper bags filled with sugared almonds and many brass bells, like the ones used to call the servants.

Nemo turned his eyes away from the lights and realised he had orientated himself well: about ten metres away from him was the place where he had fainted: the entrance hall. As he approached it, he could sense a faint smell of vinegar. A different tone of colour in the wooden floorboards indicated the place where they had scrubbed his bloodstains off. As he heard some footsteps behind him, he turned around and saw Dickson, who was coming out of the billiards room. The butler, who was carrying a tray full of wine glasses, looked at him in a peculiar way.

'Good afternoon?' Dickson pronounced the words more like a question than a greeting.

'Better than a few hours ago. That's for sure.'

'I am glad to hear that, sir.'

Nemo was a little ashamed of the dramatic way in which he had shown up a few hours ago.

'Thank you for taking me in and taking care of me.'

'There is no need to say thank you, sir. I usually pick

up everything I find on the floor,' Dickson said mockingly. 'The other... youngsters are in the...'

He didn't finish his sentence. They were startled by a gunshot. Dickson couldn't stop the glasses from jumping at the same time as him, but with a precise movement of his hand, he caught them again, and not even one drop was spilled.

The detonation was accompanied by a guffaw, which was almost as scandalous as it. When they turned around, Dickson and Nemo fixed their gaze on the eyes of the young man who had just come inside the entrance hall. He was wearing a splendid apple green coat and a cherry coloured silk tie. He was unarmed. He was carrying a box full of tubes made of cardboard and wrapped in brightly coloured paper. They were *crackers*, the latest Christmas trend in England. When two people pulled from their ends hard, the tubes were split with a loud burst, and they unloaded a little bag of presents and toys. The young man was holding the box on his knee and his hands had just burst one of the *crackers*. His Christmas spirit vanished as soon as he noticed Nemo's presence. He was as stunned as Dickson had been when he had opened the door to him. Alarmed by the expression on his face, Nemo feared that his wound might have been opened again. He took his hand to the bandage to see if it was bleeding: the bandage was dry and seemed to be in place.

'When I'm in the forest, I'm green and very tall. When they take me home, they decorate me and make me look beautiful.'

Now it was the turn for the young man with the coat to be startled, when he heard that profound voice behind him. It belonged to Clifford Ashdown, who had joined the group by surprise. He was a tall and thin young man with a mischievous expression. At any time of the day, Clifford looked as if he had just come out of bed. His uncontrollable hairs were fighting a pitched battle and all his clothes were crumpled. He was also in shirt-sleeves, without a jacket or a waistcoat, which meant a full-fledged challenge to the dress code of Victorian England. He had picked up from the floor the little piece of paper that had fallen out from the *cracker* and had read the riddle it contained, with his unmistakeable American accent. When he finished reading, he made a ball with the piece of paper and threw it at the head of the young man with the apple green coat.

'*Green. they decorate it and make it look beautiful...* It could be you, James. But you're not tall. You're rather... tiny. Then it must be the Christmas tree. And you,' he said, noticing Nemo's presence, 'must be... Memo.'

'Memo?' asked the young man of the *crackers*, with a perplexed expression.

'That clever face of yours is deceiving, James: you never know what's going on.' Clifford very much enjoyed seeing him so puzzled. 'Let me make the introductions: this is James, a great man even though he is dressed in such an unfashionable way. James, this is Memo, or Nemo, our enigmatic visitor. He came without any previous notice a few hours ago, leaving everything covered in blood. Poor Miss Marsh has spent the whole afternoon scrubbing the floor with a steel brush.'

'And how...?' James interrupted himself, not knowing very well how to ask the question.

Clifford shrugged his shoulders with a comical expression.

'Don't you know? Neither do I. And don't ask him! He has lost his memory.'

'Really?' James gave Nemo an incredulous look.

Clifford waited for confirmation from Nemo, who nodded absent-mindedly. His eyes were fixed on the American man's eyes. He was wearing baseball shoes, three sizes bigger than the ones that had left their trail on the snow in the alley. Clifford took advantage of the fact that the butler was leaving to whisper in Nemo's ear:

'He doesn't like us. Good old Dickson believes in spirits and goes once a week to a hovel in Cagliostro Street, to spend six shillings on a medium: monsieur Rouletabille. He spends hours there talking to his old fellow soldier friends from the thirty-second regiment, who died in the siege of Krishnapur. James and I have played a couple of wonderful jokes on him. We even left on his bed some ectoplasm made with pumpkin purée. By the way,' he said, turning to James, 'where have you been? I've spent the whole afternoon looking for you.'

His only reply was to show him the contents of the box that he was holding. When he saw the cardboard tubes wrapped in shiny paper, Clifford's throat let out a cascade of guttural giggles.

'Oh, ho, ho, ho.'

He sounded like a wicked Father Christmas. Without asking for permission, he took a handful with ten or twelve *crackers*, and still laughing, he turned around the corner and disappeared. Ten seconds later, the first burst could be heard, followed by the breaking of a piece of crockery, a loud cry from Miss Marsh and some footsteps rushing to get away. James gave Nemo a guilty smile.

'I've opened Pandora's box, I know. But what else could I do? We were about to die of boredom. Do you want one?'

With a gesture he offered him the box. Nemo looked at it and refused the invitation.

'You haven't got much of a Christmas spirit...'

'I must have lost it when they cracked my head open.'

'Oh. Well, we will perk you up later with some tambourines and Christmas carols. You already know Dickson. He doesn't like Clifford very much. In fact, almost everyone dislikes him. Between you and me, I don't like him either. Would you like me to introduce you to the others?'

Nemo gave James's shoes an inquisitive look. A pair of round toe ankle boots.

'Please...'

While James went ahead to show him the way, Nemo studied him carefully. He was shorter than the average man of his age, but the size of his head compensated the difference. There was a graceful imbalance between the proportionate build of his body from his feet to his neck, and the huge cranium that was on top of that.

Nemo's first impression was that those feet and that head belonged to different people. This lack of proportion made his face look magnified, and made his vivacious expressiveness even more attractive. His arms seemed strong and the raised insoles of his shoes made him tall enough to make him capable of having hit Nemo.

The young man did very well at guiding him around. He enlivened the tour with all sorts of interesting facts, both about the house and its owner.

'When I saw you with that bandage on, I thought your head had burst while you were listening to one of Crispin's monologues. Has he given you any? He's passionate about science, but he is also fascinated about paranormal phenomena. An explosive mixture. He is a great person.'

They had stopped at the end of a corridor on the second floor, in front of a walnut door, with a shiny golden handle. With a ceremonious gesture, James stepped aside, inviting Nemo to go in.

'The library…'

The wooden floor here was older than in the rest of the house. The floorboards creaked like the deck of an old sailing boat, welcoming Nemo. His eyes went around an oval room, with its walls covered with bookshelves, from the floor to the ceiling. There were about one thousand books living in good harmony in that library, hiding from humidity and dust behind some little glass doors. There was very little furniture apart from the bookshelves: a mahogany desk with drawers and some comfortable armchairs with little low tables next to them to leave the books on.

Sitting next to the desk there was a young lady, who was dipping her pen in an inkwell. She was finishing writing a letter. She didn't look up from the paper until James approached her and took the pen away from her fingers. Then she watched him in amazement, as if she had been taken out of a trance.

'Excuse my rudeness, Marie, but we've got a visitor.'

Following James's gesture, Marie found the young man with the turban.

'The stranger that Mr Crispin told us about…' she got up to shake Nemo's hand. 'Pleased to meet you. My name's Marie.'

Her blond hair was so thin that each hair turned into golden fluff at its end, dispersing the light, and creating a kind of halo around her head. Her fringe could hardly cover her wide forehead, which reminded of the visor of a medieval helmet. While the young man examined her, she x-rayed him. In her vivacious little eyes, the brightness of an extraordinarily intelligent mind could be felt. Nemo shook her hand.

'Pleased to meet you. I'm sorry I can't introduce myself. I've got absolutely no idea of who I am.'

'Don't worry. I sometimes have that same feeling.' Marie's foreign accent slightly mistreated words, but it was perfectly intelligible. 'Mr Crispin has asked us to call you…'

'Yes, I'm sorry: I'm Nemo, like Captain Nemo. I'm not sure I'm going to get used to saying that.'

'You won't have to do it. You will soon have recovered your memory. How are you feeling?'

Nemo smiled.

'I don't know. About to vomit any moment?'

'It's good to know,' James said, moving away from him a little. 'I can imagine what you are thinking: Is Marie also taking part in the competition? Why has a woman managed to join the group?' he shrugged his shoulders, with a comical gesture of resignation. 'Mr Crispin is outstanding both for his virtues and his defects. He's not only mad about spiritism, he is also a suffragist. In fact, it is almost the same thing. Have you heard about Lydia Becker?

'I know who the suffragettes are. They advocate women's right to vote.'

'Exactly. Mr Crispin not only reads their pamphlets and goes to their meetings, he also finances them!' James simulated a shiver. 'So he invited the young women from around the world to take part in the competition. Marie was not only shameless enough to accept the challenge, but it also seems that she has handed in one of the best pieces of work. Clifford isn't very happy about it.

'You must admit that you aren't very happy about it either, James,' Marie winked at Nemo. 'They can't stand the idea of a woman being more intelligent than them. If Mr Crispin gives me the prize they will plunge into the Thames, head first. I really want to win.'

Nemo showed more interest in the young lady's feet than in her scientific merits. She was wearing bulky boots that would seem appropriate for a polar explorer. Their cracked leather showed crusts of mud, thistle thorns, stains, cuts and mendings. The steel spikes on their soles would have reduced the parquet floor to splinters, if it hadn't been for the fact that every room in Mr Crispin's house was covered with thick carpets. The sole of those huge boots couldn't be any more different from the footprints he had seen in the alley. Besides, Marie was too short for her to have been able to hit him. However, from seeing her determined expression, he had no doubt that she would be able to crack open any head she wanted to.

'I was giving him a tour around the house,' James explained to Marie. 'Come on, help me. Is there anything in the library that I can show to him? Apart from the stuffed parrot.'

'Well, there's Newton's prism,' she indicated.

'Oh, that's true!' James slapped his forehead.

He pointed with his finger at a low table, in which the wood grains formed the squares of a chessboard. On it there was a stand holding a glass bar with a triangular section.

'That is thought to be one of the prisms that Sir Isaac Newton bought from the street fair in Stourbridge, in August of 1665. With it he decomposed light into a rainbow for the first time.'

Nemo took the prism from the stand and examined it.

'I very much doubt it.'

'I doubt it too, certainly, but why do you say so?'

Before answering, Nemo took a magnifying glass from the top of the desk, and used it to inspect the faces of the prism.

'It's too transparent. In Newton's period, iron impurities gave glass a greenish colour. It also had many bubbles and I can't see any here.'

'Impressive. And how do you know all that?'

'I've got no idea,' Nemo returned the prism to its place. 'I can't remember when or how I learnt it.'

'Oh, all right. Well, you shouldn't tell Mr Crispin about this. He paid five hundred pounds for the prism! Besides, even if it's fake, it does its job very well: look how beautiful it is.'

James pulled shut the curtain of the only window in the library. The room went almost completely dark. In the curtain, Gideon had cut out a little hole to let a ray of light in. When their eyes got accustomed to the darkness they saw it take shape: a golden straight line in which there were specks of dust dancing. It crossed the room until it reached the prism, and when it went through it, it was decomposed into a range of colours. A little screen, on one of the bookshelves, gathered the display of blue, green, yellow and red stripes. James pulled the curtain open, full of excitement. His eyes were gleaming.

While Marie and Nemo were blinking in silence, getting used to the light again, they heard the chiming of the bells of St Peter's church.

'Marie, I'm leaving Nemo in your hands. We'll be having dinner in half an hour's time and I need to get changed.'

'There's no need for you to get changed. You look impeccable.'

'I sure do. Now. In a few minutes' time my petunia coloured waistcoat, my striped trousers and my maroon tie will look as ridiculous as the furs of troglodytes. A gentleman should always wear a full black and white suit for dinner!'

Marie watched him as he walked away.

'I've never met anyone as vain as him. Or as intelligent. James is a genius in mathematics. He seems to have developed a method to determine the orbit of asteroids, which improves Gauss's method.' She took from the desk the letter that she hadn't finished, she folded it and put it in a pocket in her skirt. 'Come on, let's see what I can show you.'

While they were on their tour, Marie passed by a double leaf steel door, over which there was the alchemical symbol for Ouroboros, the serpent eating its own tail. The keyhole caught Nemo's attention. It had a peculiar outline: a polygon with seven sides.

'And what is this room for?'

The young woman raised her eyebrows to look enigmatic and then shrugged her shoulders.

'It's Bluebeard's room. Mr Crispin lets us go in and out of every room of the house. The only exceptions are his bedroom, the servants' bedrooms and whatever there is behind that mysterious door.'

'Everyone has their right to privacy.'

'That's what I think too.'

So Marie and Nemo left the snake and the metallic door behind. While they were looking at the collection of automatons in the music room, they were startled by another burst. They crossed Miss Marsh, who was carrying a pile of towels and rolled her eyes. Marie looked at Nemo with a questioning look.

'It's... Clifford. That's his name, isn't it? A tall and thin young man.'

Marie nodded.

'Who else could it be? And what is he doing? Has he put on his cowboy outfit and started a gunfight with somebody?'

In just a few words, Nemo told Marie about the *crackers*.

'He's one of the least funny jokers that I have had the misfortune to meet,' Marie grumbled. 'Well, we have arrived to my favourite corners of the house: the living room.'

Nemo agreed that it was the most beautiful room in the house, but it seemed a joke to him that she called it a "corner".

In fact, it was enormous. In its magnificent fireplace there was probably half of Sherwood forest burning. From the entrance, there seemed to be nothing extraordinary about the decoration, but when one paid attention to the details, nothing was what it seemed to be. Looking closely at the vanilla coloured wallpaper, it could be noticed that its drawings were not exquisite vegetable motifs, but mathematical equations, written in beautiful handwriting. The Turkish carpet showed a superb framework of molecules. The portraits on the walls weren't the faces of Crispin's ancestors looking at them, but alchemists, chemists, mathematicians and astronomers. Above the chandeliers that were hanging from the ceiling, Nemo discovered an impressive fresco that showed all the stars of the Northern hemisphere.

'All those over there, are supposed to be one of a kind,' Marie explained, pointing at the about one hundred objects that filled up the shelves, tables and glass cabinets:

there were old telescopes, astrolabes, papyrus rolls, a unicorn horn, a tortoiseshell. 'Look, those are the balls that Galileo dropped from the top of the Tower of Pisa. And there you have Franklin's kite. I suspect that more than half of them are fake.' She noticed that Nemo was looking at the miniature model of a Roman boat. 'I think it represents one of the boats that Archimedes set on fire.'

And now that we are mentioning fire, next to the fireplace, Nemo saw a freckled young man, with milky white skin and pale blond hair that reminded of recently cut hay.

He was reading in a red velvet armchair. Judging by his body posture, sitting on the edge of the seat, he seemed ready to run away at the slightest provocation. Before he noticed his presence and closed the book abruptly, Nemo could notice that its pages were full of esoteric symbols.

'Johan, I want to introduce you to Nemo.'

The young man stood up, very stiffly.

'Pleased to meet you.'

When he shook hands with him, Nemo noticed this was a cold, wet and shaky hand. It felt like holding a trout that has just been fished from a river.

Johan's extreme shyness was combined with an interesting face and a hypnotic gaze. He looked like the guardian of a terrible secret that could crush him any moment.

A strong detonation, coming from the library, made the three of them give a start.

'Oh, the stupid bast...!' Marie didn't finish the sentence, but Johan and Nemo did if for her in their own minds. 'But how many *crackers* did James give him?'

'More than half a dozen, that's for sure,' Nemo replied.

The young man discretely studied Johan's shoes. They certainly were not English shoes. They didn't have laces and they were closed with a strap and a double buckle. They didn't match the footprints in the alley either.

Clifford came running into the living room and joined them, looking back over his shoulder, as if he were being chased by a tribe of cannibals. He nearly knocked down a glass cabinet with a collection of insects in amber. After making sure that nobody was following him, he faced the disapproving expression of Johan, Marie and Nemo.

'Hey, if looks could kill, I would be instantly struck dead.

'We won't be that lucky. Don't you realise that nobody likes you?' Marie told him bluntly. 'You're the only thing I don't like about this journey and the only reason why I will be happy when it's over.'

'Thank you, Marie. That's why I do it, because I don't want you to miss me.' While he regained his breath, Clifford leaned on Johan. 'Well, Johan, have you already helped Nemo clarify his doubts?'

It was difficult to say which the most annoying thing was for Johan: the fact that Clifford had leaned on him or the fact that he had made him become the focus of attention.

'What doubts?' he asked with a frown.

Instead of answering him, Clifford turned to Nemo.

'Haven't they told you? Johan has powers.' He shook his fingers, like a spectre. 'He's a very, very powerful medium. He's the best product from Norway, after smoked salmon. If you give him a hair or a snot, he'll be able to tell you your name, your favourite colour or what size pyjamas you wear. Am I wrong?'

'Leave me alone,' Johan grumbled.

'Come on, man. Don't be shy. Use the powers that nature has given you to help this man who has no memory.'

Johan didn't answer. He kept his feverish gaze pointed at somewhere above Marie's head. Clifford was really enjoying himself.

'I challenge you to say something, just one concrete thing, about Nemo. What is his true name?, for instance. Where was he born? Does he like his T-bone steak medium rare or well-done? Has he had mumps?'

'Leave him alone, Clifford,' Marie warned him.

'No way, love. Let me remind you that this comedian is competing with us for the grant. And he's doing it in the name of science! Mr Crispin will love to know that his powers are all fake. It's all smoke and mirrors! My friend, you're automatically disqualified for the prize.'

Johan was biting his lip so hard that he seemed about to pull it off. Nemo felt uncomfortable with Clifford's aggressive talk, so he confronted him:

'So is that really what impresses you? The mind-reading show?' he asked, 'Will Mr Crispin give me the prize if I am able to read your thoughts?'

'Don't tell me you're a medium too!' Clifford watched him in amazement. 'To tell the truth, with that turban you're wearing you look as if you had just arrived from a street fair stall.'

'How much will you give me if I prove to you that I do have powers,' Nemo insisted, shaking his fingers to imitate Clifford's gesture.

'I will remain quiet… for five minutes.'

'It would be good if you did, even if it were for only three minutes!' Marie exclaimed.

With a theatrical movement, Nemo took Marie's hand by surprise and held it between his fingers. He closed his eyes. She smiled, intrigued. Clifford laughed scornfully and Johan felt relieved that the focus of attention had turned to someone else. Nemo gave his voice a profound tone, as if he were diving into Marie's mind to catch her thoughts.

'You're Polish. You usually live in Warsaw but you have been living in the country for a while, in your uncle and aunt's house. Your father is a teacher. Your mother died recently. You want to work as a chemist and the project that you are going to present to the competition has to do with explosives.

With a reflex action, Marie pulled her hand away from him. Her face had lost all its colour, and she now looked whiter than Johan. Clifford watched her, full of distrust, convinced that she had teamed up with Nemo, but the sense of deep confusion that he noticed in the young woman made him change his mind.

'How... how did you know...' Marie stammered. 'Who has told you?' She gave Clifford a furious look. 'Has it been you? Is it another one of your lousy jokes?'

'I give you my word that it isn't.'

'Your word? What word?'she said angrily, 'You probably haven't told the truth in your whole life.'

'That is true,' Clifford admitted. 'I know you are not going to believe me, but I didn't tell him anything at all. I didn't know that your father was a teacher or that your uncle and aunt lived in the country! You didn't tell us!'

'You're right... Then...'

Nemo enjoyed for a few seconds the confusion that the other three were experiencing.

'I can't believe that you're all scientists,' he finally said. 'Where do you want me to start from? Ah, how did I know that you were Polish? Anyone could tell by your accent that you weren't born in Manchester. It sounds Slavic, but my hearing is not acute enough to be able to identify your nationality. When we entered the library you were writing a letter. I couldn't manage to read a word of it, but I did notice that you added some little tails to the vowels.' With his finger, Nemo drew some letters in the air. 'The only two European languages that use them are Polish and Lithuanian, but in Lithuanian there is another symbol, the macron, which you didn't use. In conclusion: you are Polish.'

'Impressive!' They all turned their heads when they heard the exclamation from James, who had just entered the room, wearing a black tailcoat with a white shirt and waistcoat. 'No, no. Please continue, Nemo. I didn't want to interrupt you.'

'The rest is based on riskier conjectures. The main clue is the fact that you are here. How many young Polish women could have received the education required to aspire to Mr Crispin's prize? Or even to find out about its existence? Certainly not a peasant woman. It all points to a girl from the city and the only Polish city I know is Warsaw. If I've guessed that all right, it's been a bit of a fluke. And since I was thinking about a city, what kind of environment could I put you in? Judging by your appearance, and the quality of the clothes you're wearing, you're not rich. What profession could your father have had to provide you with education without spending much money? Teaching, of course!'

'And how did you know I was living in the country...?'

'Even though we are in the middle of winter, you still have a tan on your face and your skin is hardened. You must have spent a lot of time in the open air. And what do your dry hands tell me? That they have worked the land. And what is a city girl with a good education doing in the fields? Visit her family. Better her uncle and aunt than her grandparents because life expectancy is around forty years. And why would you move there? Because of the loss of someone very near to you. Your father? Your mother? A difficult choice. I have thought that for a young girl to be given permission to travel alone from Poland there must have been the intervention of a strong paternal authority.'

'And… chemistry?'

'When I took your hand I noticed that you've got a very peculiar scar. It's the mark of chemists. It's left on them when they try to push a pipette through a cork. Sometimes, when you try to do this, the pipette slides from the whole in the cork and sticks in the middle finger. It's hardly worth explaining how I found out about the explosives: you smell of gunpowder, and don't seem the kind of person who would go around dropping bombs.'

The explanations provoked some murmuring of admiration.

'Mmmhh,' Clifford grunted, and refused to give up. 'You have been lucky. That's all. Marie is too exotic. What can you say about me?'

He held out his hand to him. Nemo rejected it.

'If you don't mind, I prefer not to touch you. Your horrible accent shouts from the rooftops the fact that you're American. You like microbiology and the study of animal behaviour. Of crows, in particular. You spend a lot of time trying to train one. Its name is Poe, and it is from Virginia, the same as you.'

As Nemo spoke, Clifford's expression became increasingly tense. When he finished, he pointed at him, with an accusing finger:

'You have been nosing around my room!'

Marie laughed out loud when she saw his face and even Johan allowed himself a shy smile of revenge. Nemo enjoyed the situation for a few seconds, before proceeding to the explanations.

'Your right eye is quite irritated, much more so than the left one. I can even tell there is a circular mark around your eyelids, which proves you spend hours with your eyes on the ocular of a microscope. That's how I know about the microbiology. Although you're wearing a very crumpled shirt, I've noticed two very tiny marks of rubbing, both together, near your shoulder. They would be the marks left by the claws of a bird resting on your shoulder. That points to the fact that you spend a lot of time with a bird. Why would you take the trouble to bring her from the United States? As I see that you are very concerned about Mr Crispin's prize, I deduced that it wasn't your pet. The bird had to be related with your investigation. I know crows are the most intelligent birds.

'And how the hell do you know its name?' Clifford exploded.

'Although you consider yourself very clever, you're not very imaginative. Poe is American, just like you, and his best-known poem is titled *The Crow*.'

In order to impress them even more, Nemo hid from them who his main source of information was: Clifford himself. He had identified him as the owner of the voice he had heard when coming out of his room. Then, he had very angrily scolded someone called Poe, who was from Virginia, and had threatened with grounding it without dinner.

'Well done!' James applauded. 'And me?'

'To tell the truth, Marie already told me that you were some kind of mathematical genius. Apart from that, it seems obvious that your family is going through some financial struggles.'

James blinked a couple of times, before asking:

'Obvious? Why?'

'In just one hour, I've been able to admire two of your outfits. You wear expensive clothes, but you have worn them many times. The fabric is worn out at the elbows, the seams and the cuffs.'

James wasn't very happy about the fact that his family's misfortune was being made public, but he accepted it graciously. After all, it served him right for asking.

The four candidates for Mr Crispin's scientific competition had to yield to the fact that Nemo was very astute indeed. The young man felt radiant. Then, all of a sudden, he realized that he had made a major mistake. Instead of using his observation abilities in a discreet way, he had shown off like a peacock. The good hunter never makes his prey feel scared. Now he could be sure that his attacker would measure would be extremely careful, so as not to be identified.

When Mr Dickson announced that dinner was served, Nemo's stomach reminded him that it had been empty for hours.

CHAPTER THREE

On tenterhooks

The gothic arches that carried the weight of the ceiling and the glass stained windows gave the room the air of a medieval cathedral. The round table and the chairs, with very tall wooden backs, evoked the presence of King Arthur. However, the sovereign of the house was missing.

'Does he usually have dinner with you?' Nemo asked.

'He never misses a meal,' James nodded. 'Something terribly horrible must have happened to stop him from coming here and giving us one of his monologues.'

'He is a chatterbox,' Clifford confirmed. 'I think that this competition is nothing but an excuse for him to be surrounded by defenceless youngsters to torture with his speeches.'

'Shhhh, don't be ungrateful,' Marie reprimanded them, with a smile.

'I'm extremely grateful to him,' James excused himself, 'but that doesn't mean he isn't a little, just a little boring. Or would you like to hear, one more time, his famous anecdote about how he carved the Christmas turkey with a pair of nail scissors?

'Well, you tell us something, Nemo,' Clifford said. 'What do you do?'

'Clifford...' Marie reprimanded him.

'Sorry, it's just what I'm used to doing. It was to break the ice.'

They had just started the second course, a splendid duck stuffed with truffles, when the creak of the garden gates made the stained glass windows tremble. It was followed by the tinkling of some reins and the wheels of a vehicle sliding on the snow. The youngsters waited in suspense. None of them heard Mr Crispin's soft footsteps, so they were a little startled when they saw him appear next to the threshold, as if he were a spectre. He had already taken his coat off and had changed his boots for some slippers. On his red velvet cap there were some snowflakes that were almost completely melted.

'Hello, sorry about the delay. Oh, Nemo, you have already got up from bed. How are you feeling?'

Miss March served him a big plateful of soup. It was obvious that the problem was still affecting Mr Crispin's mood. Instead of starting one of his never-ending soliloquies, he asked them questions at random. In the end, Marie took the courage to question him.

'Do you feel all right, Mr Crispin? Has anything happened to you?'

The old man looked puzzled, looking at her face's reflection on his spoon, which was upside down.

'Anything?' The question alarmed him and he looked at the young lady with eyes so wide that instead of reminding of a chimpanzee, they reminded of an owl. 'No, no, no... nothing at all. Not at all. No, no... Well, yes. Yes, yes, yes. Something has happened. Something. Certainly. You're right. But it's not that important.'

Marie nodded with a kind and understanding expression, which invited him to continue.

'What has happened?'

'I don't want you to feel alarmed,' Mr Crispin finally said, 'but I can't hide it from you either. It's probably just joke. A very bad joke. I have received...' while he talked, he took from the pocket of his waistcoat a folded piece of paper, 'a death threat.'

His last words stopped the smile that was already starting to show in Clifford's mouth. The five young people dropped their forks, which tapped on the dishes, and it all sounded like a drumroll. He unfolded it on the tablecloth with the back of his hand, and passed it to Marie, for her to read it aloud.

"If you don't give us the idol before tomorrow at midday, Nachtali, the wandering warrior, will fall from the stars to recover his heart. And as payment, he will take part of yours."

Clifford couldn't stop his muffled laughter.

'It doesn't sound like a very serious kind of threat.'

'Doesn't it?' Crispin shrugged his shoulders, without showing whether he agreed or disagreed, while he took the piece of paper and put it back in his pocket.

'Who is Nachtali?' Johan asked, with such a low tone of voice that the others could hardly understand him.

'A god from the Arctic. He is worshipped by a small community of eskimos.'

'That's quite far away from here, isn't it?' James said, looking surprised. 'Why have they got anything against you?'

Gideon couldn't hide hiw own puzzlement when he answered:

'Apparently, I've got their god. At least part of it: his heart.'

For once, the youngsters were very eager to listen to him, but the old man was reluctant to talk. He was clearly trying to solve a doubt in his mind, which he finally did. Taking one of the candelabra from the table, he stood up.

'I will show it to you.'

They would have followed him to a catacomb, and in a certain way, they ended up in one. Their excitement grew as they saw that he was leading them through the mysterious steel door with the polygonal keyhole. Mr Crispin loosened his tie, unbuttoned the first button of his shirt and took off his neck a piece of cord from which there was a metallic piece hanging, with a long handle with a polyhedron on its end. The triangles of its faces showed grooves and protuberances. Their shape evoked in Nemo a vague memory, which he couldn't identify.

'Is it a key?' Marie asked.

'That's right,' Mr Crispin nodded, with a gesture of approval. Clifford frowned, as if they young lady had just got one step ahead of him in the competition.

Nemo felt a sudden revelation. The ball of clay that he had found is his coat pocket was a mould of the polygonal keyhole of the door to the room where Crispin kept the idol. His heart started beating faster, and his heartbeats affected his wound under the bandage. A wave of pain made him feel numb. Was he involved in the threat in some way?

Gideon inserted the metallic piece in the lock and turned it twice. The mechanism responded with a click. To open the door, the old man had to lean all his weight against it. That way the managed to get inside the room, the dimensions of which were hidden by the darkness. There were no windows, or if there were, they were closed. There was a spring mechanism to make sure the door would never remain open. When the last one to enter stopped holding it, it was shut. The only light came from the candles that Crispin was holding. It smelled of rust and the air was stuffy. They were feeling as if they had got lost inside a cave. Crispin turned his candle to left and right, quite fast, so as to make sure that they saw a glimpse of the room but not too much of it.

'The Crispins' family treasure' was the only explanation he gave.

They had a fleeting impression of polished metals and glasses, which kept in their reflections the light of the candles. As soon as Crispin stopped moving the candelabra, they were surrounded by darkness again. They followed him with uncertain footsteps, making sure they weren't left behind. After about ten steps, Gideon stopped and pointed the light at a shelf. On the middle of it, on a wooden base, they saw a piece of a mineral. It was about the size of a cherry.

'Is that the idol?' Clifford said mockingly. 'It looks like a mummified excrement.'

'It's the Purple Rock,' Crispin corrected him with an emphatic tone. 'It's been chiselled manually, using tools made of bone. In the Arctic, the Oldennui didn't have wood or metals available to make hammers or chisels. It's older than the babylonian small boards, worn out after being venerated for centuries.

'Do they really want to recover that ridiculous tiny thing?'

'For them it has a mm… sentimental value, I guess. Or symbolic value, rather. It represents the heart of their god.'

The Purple Rock was shining as if it had been sprinkled with sugar. It had an earthy appearance with countless crystal incrustations. The Oldennui had opened grooves on its surface and had chiselled some spines on it, which gave it a twisted and unsettling appearance.

'Well, he has a horrendous heart.' James contemplated the idol, fascinated. 'Now I can understand why he is such a vengeful god. Why don't you give it to them as a present? I'm sure the decoration of the room would benefit from that.'

Gideon was scandalised.

'It's an absolutely unique piece! The Purple Rock comes from outer space. Look, that crystalline cover was made when it came into contact with the atmosphere. According to the eskimos, their ancestors' ancestors saw it fall from the sky. They think that Nachtali got rid of a piece of his heart so as to guide them.

'Well,' Marie grumbled, wrinkling her forehead, 'then I can understand the fact that they are angry about someone having taken it away from them.'

'But it was them who sold it to me!' Mr Crispin exclaimed, with his big eyes about to drop out of its orbits. The alternation of light and shade provoked by the candlelights gave him an almost diabolic appearance. 'I can't understand what made them change their minds. Maybe a group of Oldennuis stole it and sold it to me without letting the others know about it… About a week ago they came to me, saying that I had to return it to them. Of course, they were not going to give me my money back. We're not talking about two or three shillings. I paid a lot of money for it… At the auction in Sotheby's, Nigel Ackroyd couldn't keep up with my bids. One thousand and five hundred! Two thousand pounds!'

'Who is Nigel Ackroyd?' Nemo asked.

'One of the most important collectors in the world of precious stones and minerals. He is also one of the biggest scoundrels. He earned a fortune with slave trade on the Gold Coast. But this time, he had to leave the place without anything, and very disappointed.' Mr Crispin shrugged his shoulders, with a mischievous expression. 'I don't feel sorry for him. This meteorite is extremely unique. Millions of years ago, Mars was hit by an asteroid, which pulled a piece of crust off its surface. That was the way in which the Purple Rock was propelled into space, and after travelling for two hundred million kilometres, it landed on Antarctica.

Nemo watched the alien rock, hypnotised by it. Its texture was almost identical to that of the stones he had found in his coat pocket. The coincidence made him feel very suspicious. Together with the money, it confirmed that he was involved in something shady. Could he be a thief at the service of a group of crazy eskimos? Or of an unscrupulous collector? Clifford had noticed his uneasiness and tried to pretend everything was all right.

'And what do you plan to do?' Marie said.

Mr Crispin took his cap off to scratch his head.

'Well, I wasn't going to do anything about it, but I made the terrible mistake of telling one of my best friends, Fabian Teal, about it. He also happens to be a sectional head at Scotland Yard. I didn't want to alarm him, but he has taken the threat very seriously. In his opinion, there is a chance that this might be the work of a crazy person. He wants me to stay in the safest room of the house and wait until the time when, according to the note, Nachtali will steal his heart away from me. He has insisted on sending me two of his best detectives tomorrow.'

Once they were back in the dining room, Mr Crispin continued his lively conversation with Marie, James and Clifford. Nemo shared Johan's tormented silence. His maharajah bandage served as an excuse to leave them. He had a terrible headache. He took one of the candles that Miss Marsh had put on a little table next to the dazzling Christmas tree and went up the stairs. When he got to his room, he turned the gas off and threw himself on the bed. He could hardly take off his shoes, curl up into a ball and cover himself with the blankets. He spent an hour with his eyes closed and his teeth clenched, so as not to shout from pain, until he ended up falling asleep, out of sheer exhaustion. He had two dreams. In one of them he was Nachtali and he was stealing Mr Crispin's heart. In the second dream he could identify the person who had attacked him in the alley, but the following day he could no longer remember who it was.

Chapter four

In suspense

When he woke up, the first light of the day was coming into the room. An ash-coloured clarity was coming in through the curtains, and it had very little power to take some colour from the objects in the room. His headache was lighter, but there was still an intense pain beating in his temples. Nemo spent the first few minutes of the morning trying to remember, but his past was still surrounded by a fog as thick as the one that blurred the silhouette of the trees in the garden, on the other side of the window.

He made sure that the stones and the money were still where he had left them, well hidden at the bottom of a decorative urn. He poured some water into a washbasin and washed his face. After drying it up, he pulled the curtains open and turned the gas on, to turn on the lamp hanging from the ceiling. He breathed deeply and watched himself closely. Now, when there was no audience in front of whom to try to look clever, what could he deduce about himself? He breathed deeply, rubbed his hands and tried to concentrate on what he was seeing. His shirt was made of

cotton, and very worn out. Had he bought it from a second-hand street vendor, or was it that the used it very often.

In any case, the possibility of him being the son of a millionaire seemed impossible. When he looked closer, he noticed some oil splashed on his chest and the inner side of his forearm. He visualised himself with a frying pan in his hand. Frying something. In England people used lard to cook. In some European countries people used oil. Those recent stains suggested that he had just come back from France, Italy, Greece or Spain. What foreign languages could he speak? He tried to speak in a different language. After a few minutes of mental block, some words finally flowed out: *La chambre jaune... La maison interdite...* He could speak French.

He looked at his pocket watch. It looked like the ones railway workers used, with a steel case. It had lost its chrome coating and was very rusty. The water had leaked into it and had left a stain of humidity on the porcelain disc with painted numbers. Following his intuition, he took the coat from the coat hook, buried his nose between the folds of the fabric and breathed in deeply. It smelt of salty water, which confirmed that he had travelled by boat. When he examined closely the collar folds, he noticed some traces of soot. It was the mark of all train passengers, especially those who travelled on third class coaches, the ones nearer to the firebox in the locomotive.

His hands had an extraordinary appearance. He could detect at least a dozen minor wounds, at different stages of healing. From the bruises on his knuckles he knew that he practised boxing, which could perhaps explain the fact that he had lost one of his back teeth. The calluses on the inside of his fingers pointed to the fact that he always held the handle of some kind of instrument very tightly. Along his index finger and thumb he found a long scratch. It looked like the mark caused by the rubbing the edge of the guard of a sword on someone's hand. Did he practise fencing frequently?

Although he hadn't washed his clothes for many days (something that seemed very obvious), he didn't notice any traces on them of the typical soot left by the air pollution in London. He had noticed it on James's coat, for instance, and on Marie's dress. Therefore, he couldn't have been in London for too long. He sat down in the armchair, leaned his nose on his fingertips and revised all the information that he had just gathered. He had come from France by boat, and from the port he had taken a train. He could box and he could fence. Did that mean he was a criminal?

He smelt the stones. They hadn't had the time to take on the salty water smell from the coat. Could they have been given to him by the person who had left him unconscious in the alley? Had he come all the way from France to steal Nachtali's heart? Had the eskimos asked him to do it? Or perhaps Nigel Ackroyd?

After putting the watch away and hiding the money and the stones in the urn again, he decided to go outside so as to clarify his ideas. In the garden there was an unpleasant silence. The only sound that could be heard was the muffled sound of his footsteps on the frost. The birds were shivering, and didn't seem to feel like singing at dawn. The chimneys from the kitchen and the living room were the only ones that were letting smoke out at that early time.

Nemo walked towards a solitary elm tree, separated from the chestnut trees, with its thin and naked branches spread out. There was snow falling around him. While he rubbed his hands, he looked up at the sky and had the feeling that the clouds that were covering it were turning into big frozen cotton flakes. The cold weather intensified the pain he was feeling in his wound, but all in all, it made him feel better. On the other side of the fence the curtain of snow falling was thicker, and it blurred the city skyline in the distance. It looked as if the pavement finished after just one metre's distance, and that beyond that there was nothing but a white curtain.

He knew he had to leave. Immediately. The warning note that Crispin had received announced that something terrible was going to happen before midday. The money that he had found in his pocket proved that he hadn't been mugged in the alley. The one hundred pounds could very well be in payment for stealing the Purple Rock, and the stones, a sample for him to be able to recognise the precious object. The footsteps indicated that his accomplice was in the mansion. The longer he stayed there, the more likely he would be to get into trouble that he might not know how to get out from. Without his memory, he was defenceless in front of Marie, Johan, James, Clifford, Dickson, Mr Crispin... Any of them could have betrayed him. He had to admit that his plan to follow the footsteps had been a complete failure.

He felt a shiver. Where could he go then? Where did people without memory go? To a charity home? To a police station? He didn't know if he had been involved in any other crimes. His heart sank when he thought about the loneliness that was awaiting him in the city, with its buildings deleted by the snow, as if it wanted to leave him trapped in Mr Crispin's mansion.

Nemo sighed. A sparrow shook its feathers in the tree above him. He was about to start walking towards the gate when he heard a voice behind him:

'Nemo?'

'Mmmhhh?' The young man turned around and saw how Marie was approaching him. Her big boots were leaving a trail in the snow.

He smiled when he recognised her.

'Have you already got up? How do you feel today?'

'I still can't remember who I am,' he answered with a very serious face. 'At least, my headache is not as strong as if my head were about to explode and scatter my brains on the floor.'

'Well, that's a beginning. Does the fact that you can't remember your past worry you?'

'Wouldn't it worry you?'

'It would worry me a lot,' Marie admitted. But I would try to see it as a sort of relief. I don't know, maybe your family was making life difficult for you, or you didn't like your friends very much, or you were tormented by something wrong you did. Now you're free. You've lost your roots, but you've also got rid of your burdens.'

'Mmmhh... Maybe,' the young man said, not sounding very convincing. 'But I prefer to know.'

'I would also prefer to know. But don't rush, Captain Nemo. You may find that you were nothing but a third-rate thief.'

The young man stared at Marie, putting himself on guard. He didn't notice in her expression any trace of double meaning.

'Or the son of a nobleman,' he replied automatically.

'Or a clown from the circus.'

Nemo laughed.

'That's all right. You win. I'm not in a hurry to find out.'

'Do you fancy breakfast? If you want to recover your memory, you should nourish that messed up brain of yours.'

Nemo hesitated. His eyes turned to the gate one more time.

'Of course,' he nodded. Deep inside him, he knew he was about to make a fatal mistake. In the end, Nemo turned his back on the city and walked back to the mansion with Marie.

When they entered the dining room, they found everyone else very agitated. Nemo guessed that they had spent the night thinking about how to welcome the terrible Nachtali. On the tablecloth there were only some crumbs, which Johan was twisting between his fingers, making some scary bread figures. Dickson took care of serving tea to Marie and Nemo, and of giving instructions for Miss Marsh to bring some more toast, eggs, bacon and lemon marmalade. James and Clifford were involved in a heated argument with Mr Crispin. Johan was listening attentively to every single word, but as usual, was keeping his opinion to himself.

'I can't ask you to do that…' Gideon was saying. He looked very worried and the white fluff showing under his cap was shaking more than usual. 'I really thank you for…'

'There's no need to say anything else, Mr Crispin,' James interrupted him, bluntly. 'We have enjoyed your hospitality for more than two weeks. It's the least we could do for you. Don't you think, Clifford? Johan?'

'Of course.'

'Without a doubt, without a doubt…'

Without a doubt, Clifford and Johan didn't share Clifford's enthusiasm.

'So we agree that the library is the safest place,' James continued. 'The detectives can position themselves next to the door and the window, keeping an eye on both points of access. I can watch the upper floor. You, Clifford, can go with Dickson to the entrance. If I see anyone approaching the house, whoever it might be, the milkman, the postman or a little kid asking for Christmas money, I will raise the alarm. I will run down the stairs, meet you here, and the three of us can face up to him. You, Johan...

James got stuck, while he tried to find an appropriate task for the young medium. He, in turn, was crushing a couple of bread figures. Clifford was about to tell one of his jokes, but Johan was faster. In his stare there was a strange certainty that ended up impressing the others.

'I know how to stop that ghost.'

Mr Crispin held his breath, obviously interested. Clifford warned him with a glance and bit his tongue. James invited him to continue.

'Come on. Tell us all about it...'

'There are three ways to stop a hostile ghost moving forward,' Johan said: 'with a sacrifice, by setting up a psychic shield or by agreeing on a defence plan with other spectres.'

'Are we talking about a human sacrifice?' Marie joined the conversation, while she spread butter on her first piece of toast.

'Of course.'

'Any volunteers?' Clifford muttered between his teeth.

Gideon rejected the idea, with his eyes open as wide as those of an eagle owl.

'Listen, we're not going to sacrifice anyone. What were the other options?'

'Agreeing on a defence plan with other spectres or setting up a psychic shield.'

'We'd better not get any more ghosts involved in this. We don't want things to get out of hand,' Crispin added, anxiously. 'That shield you were talking about, how does it work?'

'You draw a circle on the floor, around the area that you want to protect, using animal blood. Along the circumference you place seven wax figures, at equal distance intervals: they are the sentinels of the chimera. Each of them is carrying one of the seven tools from old crafts: a sickle, a shovel, a mallet, a saw, a file, a fishing hook and a pair of pincers. A medium recites a spell in the arcane language of the druids, to breathe life into them and keep them awake.'

When he finished, Johan had to face a wall of disgusted faces.

'Have you said animal blood?' Marie asked, raising her eyebrow.

'The goal is to stop a ghost, not to keep a peddler from coming in.'

'Something tells me that the peddler has already come into the house.'

James tapped his fingers on the edge of the table, with a thoughtful expression on his face.

'I don't believe in ghosts too much, to tell the truth, but it's better not to leave any front unprotected.' He looked for Mr Crispin's approval.

'All right,' Gideon said to Johan. 'Do it. I will talk to Miss Marsh immediately to ask for them to buy wax, get blood from some slaughterhouse and all the other elements that you may need.'

'And what shall I do?' Marie asked.

'You can later help Miss Marsh scrub the blood off the floor,' Clifford said.

Marie pointed at him with the knife that she was using to spread the marmalade.

'Do you also want me to scrub your blood?'

'Have you said that the library is the safest room in the house?' Nemo interrupted them. 'Wouldn't it be better to use the room that you showed us yesterday, with the steel door? That way you would also be able to keep an eye on the Purple Rock. Perhaps the phantom menace is nothing but a farce, a smoke screen in order to distract and steal the idol.'

His proposal caught the others by surprise. Mr Crispin spent half a second thinking about it. The idea of waiting for a spectre in a tightly closed room, which looked like a tomb without windows, left him breathless. James came to his help.

'I still think that the library is the perfect place. It's an area that is easy to control, and there you could spend many hours comfortably, without suffering from claustrophobia. But Nemo's suggestion makes sense. Why don't you take the meteorite with you when you're hiding? If you keep it with you at the library, under the vigilance of two policemen, we could kill two birds with one stone.'

'You're right!' he smiled. 'That's the good thing about surrounding oneself with intelligent people.'

They agreed to do that. Miss Marsh had started to clear the table when the entrance bell rang. It rang so loudly that Gideon feared that the bell could drop. He checked his pocket watch. It was ten o'clock.

'Those must be our detectives.'

The youngsters accompanied him to the entrance hall. Special detectives Bernhard Trent and Ruddy O'Connor from London's Metropolitan Police, caused an unbeatable impression. They showed the brusque manners that one would expect from men of action. Trent had sideburns as thick weeds, which crept along his cheeks and threw a bridge of hair under his nose. The giant O'Connor was a head taller than Clifford. As he entered the mansion, he took with his head the mistletoe that was hanging from the entrance. Trent and O'Connor smelt of lard, boiled potatoes and cheap tobacco. Only their physical appearance, as solid as bricks, was enough to scare an army of ghosts away.

Mr Crispin told them about the plans they had made over breakfast. Trent, who hardly moved a muscle when he heard about Johan's psychic shield, agreed on doing whatever they wanted as long as they didn't interfere with their work. After examining the distribution of the house, he made the same suggestion as Nemo: the armoured chamber seemed the safest place. Once again, James helped Mr Crispin, who was imagining himself like a mummy that has been put in its sarcophagus before time. The detectives ended up giving up. The library was almost as good an option as the other one. They determined that Gideon would lock himself up in there, as soon as the clock struck eleven o'clock. Before that, they would search the room carefully, to make sure that there was no one already hiding in it. Trent would position himself next to the door and O'Connor would keep watch of the back garden, right under the only window to the library. They were both armed. They would shoot at anyone who approached them without any good reason.

When the clocks in the house started their synchronised bell concert to mark eleven o'clock, the youngsters went in procession accompanying Mr Crispin to the library. There was among them a festive mood. They all seemed excited and having fun, as if they were going to take part in some eccentric game or to play a Christmas joke on someone.

Gideon selected a novel from one of the bookshelves: *The Mysterious Island* by Jules Verne. With it in his hand, he made himself comfortable on the cushions of his old wing armchair. Around him, Trent and O'Connor started to register the room. Influenced by their energetic display, Johan, Clifford, Marie, James and Nemo lent them a hand. They didn't leave a single corner uninspected. Not even a contortionist pygmy could have escaped their scrutiny. Trent opened the window, he checked that the bars were stable and leaned out: there was a ten metre vertical fall to the garden. When he looked up, his view was blocked by the eaves of the roof, about three metres above him. At the window opening, the wall was about sixty centimetres thick.

Nemo, James and Clifford couldn't stop thinking intensely, trying to find any weak spots that they hadn't taken into account before.

'How about if I pull the curtain shut?' James asked Trent. 'That way the room will be safer.'

The detective shrugged his shoulders.

'Well, you pull the curtain shut, then.'

After half an hour, Trent decided that it was time to finish the inspection, which was so detailed that it almost seemed ridiculous. He inspected the room one last time and nodded, satisfied.

'Perfect. You,' he pointed at O'Connor, 'go downstairs to the garden and never lose sight of the window. Mr Crispin, we are going to leave you here then. Don't open the door to anyone under any circumstance until the clock strikes one. If you need anything, get closer to the door and tell me. I'll be right on the other side, keeping guard.'

'Thank you very much, Mr Trent. Don't worry. I've never felt safer in my life. If you see me lying on the sofa when you come in, don't be alarmed. It won't be because I'm dead but because I've fallen asleep while I was reading.'

All of them laughed, except Dickson. The young guests said goodbye to their host. The last impression they got was that of Mr Crispin waving one of his skeletal hands at them. On the desk, on its base, he had placed the Purple Rock. The butler had the impression that the idol had life of its own, and that it had a malignant quality that made it capable of opening the crack that Nachtali would take advantage of, to enter the room.

Bernhard Trent was the last one to leave the room. He closed the door behind him and waited until he heard Mr Crispin turn the key from inside. They weren't able to hear his light footsteps towards the desk. They only heard the soft groaning of the springs in his wing armchair, under his weight. When she heard it, Marie felt a sudden sense of apprehension. She was afraid that she would never see him alive again. With a rough gesture, Trent sent them away.

'Go away. Now I don't want anyone poking around here until one o'clock.' He turned to Dickson. 'You should stay at the entrance hall, paying careful attention. I understand that you served in the light infantry regiment of the Duke of Cornwall.'

'Yes, sir. And I still have my old Tranter revolver.'

'Excellent. It wouldn't be a bad idea if you took it with you.'

Dickson nodded:

'Fully loaded and greased.'

A quarter of an hour later there was some unexpected shouting that set off all the alarms. Miss Marsh's voice could be heard even from the garden, where O'Connor was yawning without losing sight of the window. With his infallible instinct, Dickson was able to immediately detect where the sound was coming from and go to the rescue. In a corridor of the second floor, right above the corridor that led to the entrance hall, he found a livid Johan, who was receiving a colossal scolding from the maid.

'What's the matter, Miss Marsh?' Dickson intervened.

'This young man. He was trying to stain the Marrakech carpets with that rubbish...' The maid, with an expression of both incredulity and repulsion, was pointing at the bucket of pig's blood that Johan was proudly holding in his shaky hand.

The young man's lips were so tightly pursed that they hardly let out an indignant whisper:

'I'm following Mr Crispin's instructions.'

Dickson sighed. He agreed with Miss Marsh, but Johan was right.

'We will remove the carpets so that the young man can do his... job.'

Dickson watched, with special disgust, one of the wax sentinels that Johan had made. It was a figure about thirty centimetres tall, which represented a horrifying bald head. In the hole of its cranium there was a candle fitted, and from its mouth there was a sickle sticking out.

Nemo and James, who had also shown up, alarmed by the scandal, helped Dickson pick up the heavy carpets and put them aside. Clifford was the last one to show up. He simply smiled while he saw the others sweat, as they ran up and down the corridors with the rolled up carpets. He maliciously pointed at Nemo and Johan when he crossed Miss Marsh:

'Those two are still determined on leaving the house full of bloodstains, aren't they?'

Johan could complete his psychic shield without any further delay. At ten to twelve a trail of dry blood surrounded the library. The defence was interrupted when it reached the walls, but the circle continued outside, on the snow, making a wide arch that also protected the giant O'Connor. The experienced detective watched all the manoeuvres of the young medium without changing his facial expression. He didn't even get nervous when he cleared his throat to recite a spell that would awaken the sentinels and would keep them on guard against Nachtali. He shouted words without meaning while he went around and around the circuit of figures, coming in and out of the house, with a tone of voice that was at the same time scary and hypnotic.

'Good job,' Clifford praised him, as he saw him appear with an open book in his hand, howling in a trance. 'If I were Nachtali, I would prefer to go without my heart rather than having to hear your shouting.'

Johan ignored him. James revised all the preparations.

'We have checked that the library was empty. We have even looked under the vases! The window is tightly shut, it has bars outside, and we have also pulled the curtain shut. Mr Trent is guarding the door, and O'Connor the garden. The room is inaccessible, unless someone tries to come in through the floor or the ceiling. I will watch the esplanade in front of the house from the second floor. Johan has set up a… parapsychic shield with seven horrible wax figures. Dickson and Clifford are guarding the entrance. It's perfect!' he exclaimed, satisfied. 'It's absolutely impossible for anyone to enter and try to harm Mr Crispin.'

Clifford, Nemo and Marie had to agree with him. When Johan's chanting, which was following them like a storm on the background, was interrupted, they were almost startled. A draft of air must have blown out the candle he was using to light the book. James took his hands to his pockets, very nervous, as if he feared that the shield could be ruined by the interruption:

'Hurry up. Has anyone got a light?'

Nemo didn't have any matches on him, but he took a piece of paper that he found in his jacket. He looked at the others suspiciously. When was the last time that he had checked his pockets? He couldn't remember it. Anyone could have put the note in one of them without him knowing it. He stepped aside to read it discreetly. It contained a very short message: "I know who you are. If you want to know all the answers wait for me at the greenhouse in five minutes' time."

Before he finished reading, his heart started pounding.

'And what are you doing?' James asked Marie.

'While you have fun with your little manly things, I'm going to Mr Crispin's laboratory. I don't think Nachtali's spirit will show up, to tell the truth. And I've got a very important experiment to finish.'

'And you, Nemo? Don't you want to come with me while I keep guard?'

'I've got a terrible headache,' the young man excused himself. 'I think I'm going to lie down for a while. If Nachtali shows up, don't bother to tell me. I don't feel like meeting him at all.

He pretended to be going to his room, but as soon as he lost sight of the others, he changed the direction of his footsteps. After all the hustle and bustle of the preparations, the absolute calm that could be felt at the back of the house immersed him in an atmosphere of unreality. A yard covered in snow separated the main building from the greenhouse. Once inside, the young man felt like an investigator in a remote polar station, carrying out some kind of botanical experiment. The drops from the condensation that adorned the glass walls blurred his view of the outside. There were big palm trees, which were bent and touching the ceiling of the greenhouse. The plants were distributed into rows, but the exuberance of the cycads and ferns was making them grow out of their plant pots. A profusion of leaves and stems was blocking his view, but Nemo had the impression that there was no one waiting for him there. Not yet. A light creak put him on guard. It came from some undetermined place, in front of him. Could there be anyone hiding behind the tropical plants? He picked up a spade as if it were a sword and walked forward, one step, two… He turned into another corridor and then turned left and right fast. There was no one. He felt the air tremble and turned around immediately. Too late. There was a body coming towards him. He instinctively dropped the spade and protected himself with his hands. Something hit him on his arms… not very heavily.

With his heart pounding, as it were going to jump out from his mouth, he smiled:

'Poe.'

Sure enough, a beautiful crow, extremely black and bad tempered, was flapping its wings in front of him. The bird crossed the greenhouse like an arrow and disappeared into the garden with a croak of complaint.

Nemo let himself drop on a sack of earth. "How silly of me to be scared like that", he thought, while he slowly recovered his calm. He checked his railway-man pocket watch. It was a minute before twelve o'clock. His desire to know his own identity had blinded him. Now he was convinced that no one would show up for the date. He had been the victim of a manoeuvre to take him out of the house. In the perfect silence of the greenhouse, he could hear the ringing of the entrance doorbell. It rang for a second time. After all, someone had shown up. For a few seconds he doubted whether to stay there waiting or to go back to the house. Then he clearly heard the sound of a gunshot. Nemo immediately stood up and ran to the library. With all the hurry, he knocked over many plant pots with orchids, and he even pulled a climbing plant off the ceiling. As he left behind doors, corridors and flights of stairs, he started to realise that it didn't matter how fast he went: he was going to get there too late anyway.

Chapter five

In a trance

During the siege of Krishnapur, Dickson had had the chance to become accustomed to keeping his calm. He accepted Clifford's company, who for the first time seemed to be willing to do something different from joking. The young man had stayed behind him, at a prudent distance, next to the Christmas tree. When Dickson heard the doorbell ring, he was standing in front of the entrance door. He was a little startled, because he hadn't heard the creak of the gate outside, or the footsteps on the gravel path. It was as if a ghost had materialised under the mistletoe, on the other side of the door. He clenched his teeth and combed his eyebrows. The doorbell rang again, with impertinent insistence. Dickson, decisively, took a couple of footsteps forward. In the right pocket of his uniform he had his old Tranter. His left hand, which was covered in a glove, held the door handle while his right hand took the gun and slid a finger to the trigger. He turned the door handle, breathed deeply, sharpened his stare and opened the door with a quick movement. He was prepared to face anything... anything, except what he found, which was... absolutely nothing.

In front of him, the empty esplanade descended on a soft slope towards the gate. In the thick snow that had been piling up since the beginning of the day, there was no sign of footsteps. Perplexed, and still extremely cautious, the butler looked around and kept his attention on the doorbell. It had been heavily rung, he was sure of that.

After that, his eyes swept the whole area, from left to right. There was no one to be seen. The distance between the door and each of the ends of the main façade was about thirty metres. He had walked along that distance hundreds, maybe thousands of times. Scarcely ten seconds had passed from the moment when the bell had rung until the moment when he had opened the door. In that really short interval nobody would have been able to run away from there, turn around the corner or hide in the chestnuts. And certainly no one could have done any of those things without leaving any footprints!

Clifford's voice, behind him, startled him. His incoherent words expressed a profound and primitive fear.

'Footsteps! *The spirit!*'

Dickson spent a few seconds blinking, without understanding him. And then, indeed, he heard some footsteps in the corridor, *but there was nobody in the corridor*. He saw a horrified look on Clifford's face, who was about to faint.

'Let's follow them! They're going to the library!' the butler determinedly exclaimed.

Clifford and Dickson then started a demented race, trying to follow and invisible creature that was running up the corridor extremely fast. The only proof of its presence was the sound of its footsteps, which they could hear in front of them, touching the ground with some non-physical feet. Dickson didn't stop looking at the floor, trying to see the footprints on its surface. And the truth is he thought he was seeing them. At the bottom of the big staircase they ran over Johan. With the bump, his book of spells jumped out of his hands and ended up in a fishbowl.

'The shield, the shield will resist,' he managed to say, before standing up and running up the stairs, after them. When they reached the second floor they were about to bump into Marie and James, who were also running towards the library.

'What's the matter?' Dickson asked them hurriedly.

'I don't know,' Marie said, pointing at James. 'He's started pounding at the door to the laboratory, as if he had gone crazy, and...

'I saw an old man... an eskimo... on the esplanade,' James explained, panting. He rang the doorbell. Did you open the door for him?'

'An eskimo?' Dickson clenched his teeth so hard that he was afraid that they could fly out of his mouth. 'When I opened the door there was nobody!'

'So then he has come in!' Johan exclaimed, out of breath.

'Can you hear his footsteps?'

'I can't hear anything!'

'He must be in the library by now.'

When he saw them all turn around the corner, Bernhard Trent, who had been keeping guard in the same position since they had left them there, had an astonished expression on his face. He stopped them with an imperative gesture.

'Stop right where you are,' he warned them, pointing at them with his revolver. 'What's the matter? What's all this fuss about?'

They were about to start a series of rushed explanations when they were interrupted by some noises coming from inside the library.

The sound of the wing armchair being smashed on the wooden floor shook them as if they had received an electric shock.

'He is already inside!'

Johan's teeth were clicking and his voice was trembling:

'*He has broken the shield…*'

Through the door they could hear Mr Crispin's muffled screams:

'Help! Open the door! For goodness…'

A gunshot could be heard that left them frozen. To tell the truth, Trent was the only one able to keep his calm. He forced the golden door handle, but it was locked.

'Gideon! Can you hear me? I'm Bernhard Trent. Open the door!'

The only answer he got was a terrible silence. Trent waited for only three seconds. He made the others step aside, he took a few steps back to gain some impulse and threw himself onto the door. The thick chestnut door resisted once and again. It was at that moment when Nemo appeared, flushed from his run from the greenhouse. He immediately took care of the situation and pointed at a piece of furniture in the corridor:

'The bench.'

Trent, Dickson and Nemo joined their efforts to lift up the heavy wooden bench and used it as a battering rum. At the third attempt, the door jumped out of its frame.

They felt as if they were going into Tutankhamun's funerary chamber. With all the fighting there had been inside, the lamp of the desk had fallen on the floor, and it was off. The room had become completely dark except for the light blade that came in through the hole in the curtain. This time it wasn't decomposed into a rainbow and it drew a bright circle on the wall, between the two bookcases. The clarity from the corridor was poured into the room, and let them see the corner of a carpet and a shoe. Trent rushed to take it, while James immediately pulled the curtain open.

They had only spent a few seconds in the darkness, but when the light of the day came into the library, they blinked with a sense of confusion, as if they had just been woken up from some profound sleep.

Before their eyes there was a terrible scene. Gideon's body lay on the carpet, motionless. Around him there were a few objects scattered on the floor: a copy of *The Mysterious Island*, a broken porcelain ashtray, the base of the Purple Rock, a glass paperweight, the armchair, turned upside down, a clothes peg… They all felt some sort of supernatural tension. A diabolic presence was poisoning the familiar atmosphere of the library.

They heard O'Connor's loud voice from the garden, asking what had happened. Trent, Nemo and Dickson had been the first to enter. James, Clifford and Marie had followed them. Johan hadn't dared to cross the threshold and had stayed there, holding onto the door frame.

Trent loosened Crispin's tie to help him breathe. They were horrified when they noticed that on his shirt, there was a bloodstain. They then realised that there was a strong smell of gunpowder in the room. In the still air, next to the chess door with the prism, they managed to see the last curls of blue smoke floating in the air before they vanished.

Everyone's looks turned to Mr Crispin.

'Is he...?' Marie asked.

Trent used his index finger to try to find the old man's jugular.

'He's alive.'

Six sighs of relief could be heard in the library. Mr Crispin's arteries hardly received any blood to lend colour to his livid face. Now he didn't look like a chimpanzee but simply like a skull. A skull that still had two huge eyes, widely open, paralysed by some terrifying sight. His pupils had widened to their fullest to look at a ghost, or perhaps at death itself.

They were watching the old millionaire so closely that they ended up noticing his weak breathing, which made his chest move lightly up and down. After making sure he was alive, Trent took his revolver and looked around with a wolf stare. Johan was still holding onto the door frame, so nobody could leave the room without him noticing it.

'He's still in here,' Trent mumbled.

A shiver went up the spines of the five youngsters. Their eyes went automatically from Gideon, to making an anxious and exhaustive search of the room.

Trent, Dickson and Nemo looked behind the bookcases and under each table and armchair. Finally, feeling disoriented, they started to inspect the corners where it seemed absurd that a person, however small, could have hidden in: the case of the pendulum clock, the glass cabinets full of books… even the drawers of the desk! When Trent spoke again he looked as puzzled as one can ever be.

'There is nobody,' he was forced to admit.

The supernatural feeling reached its climax. Their looks came and went, obsessively, from the door to the window. They had had to knock down the door! Nobody could have escaped through the entrance. The window, behind the curtain, was hermetically closed, and its intact bars could be seen through it.

At that moment O'Connor, panting, made his way into the room, next to Johan, and took them out of their amazement.

'What has…?'

Trent couldn't find a reasonable explanation to give him, so he interrupted him with an authoritarian:

'Call a doctor!'

O'Connor disappeared as fast as he had arrived. Trent pulled Gideon's shirt and waistcoat open, to look at his chest. In spite of the bloodstain he couldn't find any traces of wounds. Then he tried to make the old man speak. He seemed to be in a state of shock. The only thing he could make him say was a series of mumbles, impossible to understand.

'Dark… dark… The hollow man… He came flying… The heart… My heart!'

Trent, still on his knees, was watching the others' movements out of the corner of his eyes.

'Don't touch anything,' he warned them. 'I don't want anyone to come in or out of this room. Have you heard me well? Nobody! You, come in.'

He was talking to Johan, who obeyed him, alarmed.

'The idol has disappeared,' Nemo informed, as he watched its base lying on the floor.

'The threat has been fulfilled!' Johan said in a terrified low voice. 'The creature has recovered its heart.'

At that moment O'Connor returned.

'Doctor Thorndyke is coming. I've also informed our Head Office.'

Trent quickly put him up to date.

'There has been a robbery. Don't let any of these brats leave.'

The first reaction that Marie, James, Nemo, Johan and Clifford felt was one of indignation, but they didn't say a word. Given the circumstances it seemed natural that they could be considered suspects. Trent and O'Connor methodically registered Crispin, as delicately as they could, to make sure that the millionaire hadn't kept the meteorite in a pocket of his trousers or his jacket.

'Nothing,' O'Connor sighed.

'I'm going to take him out and put him on a bed,' Trent informed him.

Gideon weighed little more than a pillow stuffed with feathers, and the detective carried him in his arms without effort. The only reaction from the old man was to open his lips and moan:

'The man… the young man… The hollow man!'

'A glass of brandy would do him good,' James suggested. 'To revive him.'

Trent nodded. Johan, who was standing next to the cocktail cabinet, took a bottle of brandy and gave it to the detective, who was already at the door.

'You stay here, keeping guard,' Trent ordered O'Connor. 'Make sure that nobody comes in our out of the room, not even mice or bacteria.'

Marie, Johan, Clifford, James, Nemo and Dickson remained in the library, with the Irish giant keeping an eye on them. Each of them felt knocked out in their own way.

Dickson, who had been able to face the guns of the sepoys without getting nervous, was still petrified, as if Nachtali hadn't left the room and still were in there watching every single thing they did.

Johan seemed overcome by the same fear. He was trying to remember a thousand spells to send ghosts away, and was obsessively muttering them to himself.

O'Connor was unsuccessfully trying to fight against his sleepiness.

Marie, James and Clifford were trying to overcome a kind of mental short-circuit. Their scientific minds were facing the unexplainable. A ghost had knocked on the door to the mansion, had squeezed in between Dickson and Clifford, run ahead of them, vanished, gone through the walls of the library, shot at poor Mr Crispin, recovered the Purple Rock, and had vanished with it, without Trent and O'Connor having seen anything.

'The shield didn't work,' Johan lamented. He was nervously playing with the buttons of his jacket. One of them ended up flying out of it and rolled on the carpet. Johan watched it terrified.

Clifford, in a very bad mood, stared at him with an angry expression:

'Are you surprised? Your pathetic tricks couldn't have stopped even a three year old kid!'

'Not so pathetic,' James corrected him, picking up the button and giving it back to Johan. 'Something has happened here...'

He didn't know how to end the sentence.

'Something supernatural?' Marie helped him, with an incredulous expression. James shrugged his shoulders.

'Ah, come on!' Clifford protested. 'You've tightened your tie too much, because you're obsessed with your looks, and your blood isn't getting to your head. Let me remind you that we are here because of a contest that rewards our scientific efforts. You should be disqualified, simply for thinking about those things.'

'Relax, Clifford,' Marie grunted. 'And stop thinking about the prize at once. Mr Crispin is on his way to hospital!'

James replied:

'Until fifteen minutes ago I couldn't have agreed with you more, Clifford. But I've got eyes. I saw that old man in the snow. I saw him...'

'There was nobody,' Dickson muttered, while he tried to get out from his trance.

James ignored him:

'Mr Crispin was safe and sound and with the Purple Rock, guarded by two policemen in a tightly locked room. Trent and O'Connor had inspected everything, inch by inch and we have had to knock the door down to enter. And in spite of all that, look at what's happened,' Johan followed the movement of his lips, hypnotised. 'We heard Mr Crispin asking for help, we heard the fighting and the gunshot. And there's nobody in here! I can only see a cloud of gunpowder. Nothing else! I can't even see a gun!'

The only one who didn't seem to be under the influence of ghosts was Nemo, who was interestedly looking at some books from a bookshelf. Marie followed his eyes and on the pink leather spines she recognised a French collection of romantic novels.

'Do you miss a little bit of romance?' she asked him, with a reproachful tone. Nemo's calm attitude seemed completely out of place at a time when Gideon could be fighting to remain alive.

'Well, the topic is not very appealing to me. No, I was just looking at the bullet.'

Everyone's faces, except O'Connor's (who was about to fall asleep), turned to Nemo. Indeed, on the bookshelf that the young man with the turban was inspecting, a bullet had perforated the glass of the glass cabinet, and had got incrusted in a thick book titled *The Game of the Daisy*.

'But I don't understand!' James said, in despair. 'Where's the gun?'

Nemo turned around, as if he were trying to follow with his imagination the trajectory of the bullet. While he did this, his eyes crossed those of Marie. Nemo's mind had completely recovered from the strike on his head, and was working at full steam. He didn't even feel a trace of the pain on the back of his neck that had become permanent since the day before.

He registered every detail of the room as if he were a photographic camera. Taking advantage of the fact that O'Connor had fallen asleep, leaning on the door frame, he studied the mechanism of all the clocks. Dickson, Clifford, James, Marie and Johan looked at each other, remembering Trent's warning not to touch anything.

Finally, Nemo squatted down next to the elements that Mr Crispin had thrown on the floor, when he was fighting with the ghost: *The Mysterious Island*, the wing armchair, the stand, a pen, a broken and blackened porcelain ashtray… He was going to take the looking glass, but he couldn't find it on the desk. It was on a shelf, behind James. He had to move him aside a little to take it.

'Sorry.'

He was inspecting the stains on the ashtray, when a stranger appeared at the threshold to the library. When hearing his footsteps, O'Connor had woken up and stepped aside to let him pass, with a brusque but respectful gesture.

'What a mess,' the stranger sighed.

'Inspector…' O'Connor said as he stood at attention.

The newly arrived accepted the greeting without even stopping, with a cough.

'O'Connor…'

Inspector Appleby had a delicate and distracted air, but nothing escaped his half-closed eyes, and was able to knock a medium-weight down with just one left hook. The first thing that caught his attention was the beautiful tiepin that James was wearing. He took a mental note: "Tomorrow I'm going to buy one like that. It combines perfectly well with my peach coloured waistcoat." Then he looked attentively at Marie, Clifford, Johan and Nemo.

'Children,' he grumbled.

Dickson took him more seriously and slightly bowed his head to him.

'I am Cyril Appleby, Scotland Yard Inspector,' he announced. 'I represent law and order, and that's precisely what I've come here to do: to impose order and make sure that the law is enforced. They have taken Mr Crispin into Charing Cross Hospital. He's out of danger. That's all I'm going to tell you about that. From now on I will be asking all the questions. Mr Crispin in suffering from hallucinatory delirium and he won't say anything other than stories about ghosts and eskimos. For the time being, that will not be my working hypothesis. What we officially know about what's happened here is that there have been an attempted murder and a robbery.

Appleby stopped, admiring how well his baritone voice was sounding. "I do my job extremely well", he thought. He shook off an imaginary speck of dust from his trousers before he went on:

'I will tell you what we are going to do. This friendly gentleman here is Sergeant Carrados.'

He pointed at a policeman wearing a uniform, who was entering the room at that precise moment. More than friendly, the sergeant looked grumpy and unpleasant.

'He will search you very carefully. If you have on you even something as small as lice, he will be able to find it. As soon as he is finished with each of you, you will go to the living room, where O'Connor will keep you company. Don't move from there unless there is an earthquake, a meteorite collides against the mansion or I personally tell you to do it. Do you understand? I will call you one by one to interrogate you. When I finish, at about six o'clock, I expect to have solved this messed up case. I've got to go to the theatre at seven o'clock.'

'And what are you going to watch?' Clifford asked, defiantly.

'*The Hunchbacked Man's Slippers*.'

'I've heard it's a really bad play,' James commented.

Appleby didn't show any sign of reaction to his comment:

'Better then, I'm hoping to be fast asleep by the time of the interval.' He looked at Carrados. 'Let's start.'

Carrados caught his attention by clearing his throat and pointed at Marie with his head.

'Start with the others. I will ask for Mrs Orcy to come here and take care of her.'

Chapter six

In danger

The events took place exactly the way Inspector Appleby had announced to them. Sergeant Carrados checked them without hesitation. If they had hidden the idol in their mouths, in their shoes or in some other even more recondite place, he would have found it. Each element that he found, whether it was a used handkerchief, a penny or a grain of sand, he put in a cardboard box, which had its owner's name on top. When he finished his search, he sealed the box and they were sent to the living room. The last one to arrive was Marie. They waited there until Appleby called them.

As the inspector gathered information, his confident face was becoming more sombre. After nine interrogations he had filled his notepad with incoherent facts. With his arms folded, he looked perplexedly at the bullet incrusted in *The Game of the Daisy*. Then his eyes surveyed the objects scattered on the floor, the door knocked out of its frame, the hermetically closed window... Mr Crispin was a close friend of Superintendent Teal's, so that case was for

Appleby what we usually know as a hot potato. His superiors wanted immediate results. If the Purple Rock didn't appear in a matter of hours, no one would be happy with the story of an avenging god who had come all the way from Laponia to recover his heart.

While the inspector checked his notes, two of his best agents were turning the library upside down, looking for the idol. They lifted up the carpets and put them aside. They disassembled each of the pieces of furniture, emptied the vases, took all the books out of the bookcases, and moved these aside. There wasn't a single corner in the room that escaped their scrutiny. They measured the room millimetre by millimetre and compared its dimensions to those of the rest of the house, so as to discard the existence of a secret chamber, or some hidden place behind the walls. They went up a ladder to examine the lamp globes. With a mallet, they hit every centimetre on the floor to make sure it was completely solid. The room didn't have a fireplace, but was heated by draught of hot air coming from the fireplace in the kitchen downstairs. They examined each floorboard and made sure that none of them covered a hollow space where the idol could be kept. Finally, they shook their hands, which were full of dust and dirt, and shrugged their shoulders: there was nothing there.

Appleby sighed and nodded with resignation. He had put his trust in Trent and his search of Crispin, before he had been taken out of the library.

O'Connor could certify that no decrepit eskimo had been seen in the garden.

Finally, Carrados had examined the brats with his usual perfectionism. Appleby doubted even less Trent's report. He was convinced that at eleven o'clock that morning, before

closing the door and saying goodbye to Mr Crispin, the Purple Rock had been lying on its wooden stand, on the desk. Another sigh, bigger than the first one, escaped from his chest. He had to admit that all those facts didn't make any sense. How could he explain the invisible being that Clifford and Dickson had chased? And how had anyone managed to reach that room that was carefully guarded by his men? For one moment he contemplated the possibility that Nachtali could have fulfilled his revenge; that he had vanished after doing that. His only hope to come out from that mess was that enigmatic young man: Nemo.

Appleby had always been distrustful of people who told him about their bad memory during their interrogation. But saying he had amnesia had been too much. He hadn't believed a single word of his story. He was the only one who didn't have a good reason to be at Crispin's mansion. The inspector's instinct and experience pointed at him as the person to blame, and Appleby was very rarely wrong. He left his notepad aside and asked for Nemo's room to be carefully searched.

* * *

The interrogations continued in the afternoon. Mrs Sayers was given permission to make sandwiches and they all had lunch together in the living room, in spite of not feeling hungry at all. The space around the fireplace had become an improvised waiting room. They came in and out, escorted by Trent or Carrados, on their way to the library, where Appleby was waiting for them, sitting on the edge of the desk, with his notepad open. When he closed it, they went back to the living room.

Everyone was extremely nervous. Miss Marsh was wringing her hands and drying them on her apron, once and again, trying hard to resist her intense urge to cry. Dickson was feeding the fire with the same expression with which he would have waited for the verdict of a court-martial. The youngsters' faces were also a pitiful sight. Each one was ruminating what had happened in their own way, but they all shared a combination of unsettlement and anxiety. With the passing hours, they also felt increasingly fed up.

'Don't these people ever rest?' Clifford finally complained. They had been hearing all sorts of bangs and mallet blows coming from the library for a long while.

'They want to recover the idol,' Nemo answered. 'The first few hours are crucial to prevent the stolen object from disappearing.'

'And how do you know that?' Clifford asked him bluntly. 'Or is it that you have been personally involved in many robberies?'

Nemo looked away, confused. He knew it, but he didn't know how or why he knew it. In any case, Clifford was right. What if he knew it because he had taken part in other robberies? Or even worse: what if he had taken part in this one and just couldn't remember it? Nemo measured with his footsteps the space between the glass cabinets. His interrogation with Appleby hadn't turned out well. It was obvious that he considered him the main suspect. Sooner or later they would search his room. Would they find the money and the stones inside the urn? If they did, his situation was going to look really bad. He should have got rid of them. Why had he been so careless? He should have left early that morning, while he was still in time!

He heard the ticking of the clock on the mantelpiece, above the fireplace. Appleby could appear at any moment asking him for explanations. He watched the others. Someone in that room knew who he was. Someone who had stolen the meteorite in front of him. And if he didn't do something about it fast, he was going to end up carrying the can. His blank mind left him at everybody else's mercy. Not only the thief, but also the police and the justice system.

If Appleby couldn't solve the mystery, he would blame it all on him. Nobody would accept an unsolved case about ghosts which would make Scotland Yard look ridiculous. The stones and the money would be enough to incriminate Nemo. He felt the cold sweat soaking his back as he thought about the possibility of going to prison. Who would come to his defence? He couldn't turn to his family or friends... He didn't know who they were or where they lived! He was alone. He clenched his teeth. His only way out was to find out what had happened and unmask the criminal before they accused him. He had to think. He panicked as he felt a storm being formed in his mind. The pain from the wound was beating in the back of his neck, under the bandage. It had started as a deaf rumour, but now it was growing into waves, and expanding to the rest of his head, disturbing each and every one of his thoughts. However difficult it was, he had to concentrate. His future was at stake.

He turned to Clifford.

'What happened at the entrance hall, before we met at the door to the library? Mr Appleby asked me if I had seen anything, but I was in the greenhouse. I only heard the ringing of the doorbell, and then the gunshot.'

Clifford didn't seem to be willing to give explanations to anyone who wasn't a police officer.

'Come on, Clifford, don't try to look mysterious,' he was urged by Marie, who was bored to death.

Clifford answered, reluctantly:

'The entrance doorbell rang. Dickson was going to open the door, but when he did… there was nobody in the garden.'

'What do you mean by "nobody"?' James reacted. 'I saw an eskimo from the window upstairs!'

'When I say nobody, I mean nobody,' Clifford said, with an offended tone. 'Dickson looked out and from the doormat to the gate, which was a hundred metres away, nobody could be seen. The esplanade of snow that surrounds the house was intact. There wasn't even a single footprint. If a robin had stood on it, it would have left its footprints, and we would have seen them. If you don't want to believe me, ask Dickson!'

The butler was poking the fire in the fireplace. He was lost in his own thoughts, crushed under the weight of a heavy commotion, but he finally managed to nod very slowly.

'There was nobody.'

'It could have been one of your trained birds,' Marie suggested, as she thought aloud.

Clifford jumped angrily.

'What do you mean?' he asked her with a distrustful tone of voice.

'What? I'm only mentioning a possibility. Who could ring a doorbell without leaving any footprints? Someone who doesn't step on the floor… A bird. It could have shaken it with the bell with its beak.'

'That's ridiculous,' Clifford barked, with a congested face. 'Poe was in its cage, in my room, I haven't trained him to ring any bell.'

'All right, all right, calm down. I'm not saying that you ordered it to do it. No one is accusing you.'

'Well that's what it looks like!'

'And what happened after the ringing of the doorbell?' Nemo insisted.

Clifford tried to calm down. He realised that his attitude was starting to look suspicious to the others. Before resuming his narration, he turned his look to the floor again:

'We felt some footsteps in the corridor,' he said without much enthusiasm.

'What do you mean by "felt"?'

'What I have just said! We felt someone running in the corridor. But we couldn't see him. We could only hear his footsteps. And we followed them. They were echoing right in front of us.' When he saw Marie's incredulous expression, Clifford asked for Dickson's confirmation one more time.

'It's the way he says.'

'There must be some explanation,' Marie muttered, denying with her head.

'I felt something too,' Johan said. They all turned to him, startled by his low tone of voice. They had almost forgotten that he was there.

'I saw, with the same clarity that I'm seeing you now, an eskimo crossing the esplanade,' James admitted, unwillingly. 'He looked like a dead man who had just come out of his tomb, with some purple marks around his eyes.'

Dickson, Miss Marsh and Johan trembled. Nemo turned to Marie.

'What were you doing?'

'I was working in the laboratory when, all of a sudden, James came in, looking extremely nervous. He caught me with a bottle of sulphuric acid in my hand and I nearly dropped it all on me. He shouted at me that we had to run to the library. That there was something happening there. We left in a rush and bumped into Dickson and Clifford.'

'There's only you missing,' Nemo pointed at Johan with his finger. 'Where were you?'

'I was... I was at the bottom of the stairs, closing the spell.'

'Well, you left something open, didn't you?' Clifford said mockingly. 'Because a ghost did escape your supervision and entered the house.'

'I thought you didn't believe in ghosts,' Johan replied dryly.

'And I still don't!'

'It must have been an animal...' Marie insisted.

'Someone in your family, perhaps?' Clifford replied.

'I'm not accusing you,' Marie tried to calm him down, 'but someone entered the library. It was impossible even for an ant to go through the door that Trent was guarding: you had to knock it down. And who else but a bird could have flown to ring the doorbell without leaving any footprints or go into the library through the window?'

'The window was tightly closed,' James replied. 'It was perfectly fitted in its frame and it was also bolted.'

Nemo agreed:

'I myself saw how Trent bolted it.'

Marie didn't give up:

'Even so, it had to be through the window. Perhaps Mr Crispin opened it at some point, soon before twelve o'clock. Do you remember his last words?: "Dark... dark... He came flying". I'd say it's a crow.'

'A bird couldn't have shot at Mr Crispin, Marie,' James objected.

'It's absurd!' Clifford exclaimed.

'And what if it was the other way round?' Marie insisted. What if it was Mr Crispin who shot at the bird? He is a very impressionable person. Perhaps being confined in the library made him anxious. It was dark, with the curtain pulled shut and it was getting near the time for Nachtali's expected attack. He panicked and ran to the window to get some fresh air. The last thing he could expect at that moment was that a bird would throw itself onto him. He started to shout like a madman while he tried to take it off him. He threw all the objects on the desk, turned the armchair upside down and shot at what he thought to be a spirit. The gun fell on the floor and the bird flew away with it. Crows like shiny objects, don't they? It all happened so fast that Mr Crispin didn't get to know who had attacked him. He only had enough time to close the window again to avoid a new aggression. The shock was so strong that he then fainted.'

James looked at the tip of his shoe while he shook his head.

'You're forgetting many details, Marie.'

'Let's see...'

'The Purple Rock also disappeared. It's not a shiny object, and I think it's too much to ask for the bird to carry the gun in its feet and the idol in its beak. Then there was the bloodstain on Mr Crispin's shirt, which the bird couldn't have caused him. And to end up, even if it had rung the doorbell, how can you explain the footsteps that Dickson and Clifford heard in the corridor? And the eskimo that I saw?'

Marie remained uncertain for a few seconds, about to answer him. But she didn't say anything.

'James is right,' Nemo granted, 'but I like your theory very much.'

'What do you like about it?' Clifford grunted. 'The fact that there is a bird in it? It's ridiculous!'

'I think it is a good attempt to solve an impossible mystery. She has nearly, nearly, managed to do it. This proves that we can find a rational explanation without talking about ghosts. You do nothing but complain.'

'And you do nothing but ask questions. Who do you think you are? Appleby's cousin?'

'I'm only trying to understand. Isn't that what you scientists are supposed to do?'

A sound of footsteps distracted their attention. The round of interrogations had just finished with Mrs Sayers, who entered the room, with a pale face, escorted by Cyril Appleby and Sergeant Carrados. The inspector's entering the room imposed a complete silence that became even thicker when seconds passed without him saying anything. Appleby was behaving as if there were nobody else in the room. In fact, he was using one of his usual tactics. He was trying to make them nervous, because a guilty person who is also nervous, is very likely to betray himself or herself. While he avoided everyone's stares and walked up and down the living room, tapping his chin with the notepad, Carrados carried out his instructions to pay close attention to their reactions. The cook and Johan were about to have a heart attack. Dickson was still motionless, leaning on the fireplace, although he was probably almost getting burnt.

James and Marie were patiently waiting for the inspector's evolutions. Clifford looked indignant, as if the situation were an insult to his honour, and kept his eyes fixed on the designs on the carpet. Nemo watched with incongruent interest the miniature model of a Roman boat in one of the glass cabinets.

Appleby counted on the fact that everyone would be watching every single move he made. At a moment that he had precisely calculated, he turned around to face them, while he closed his notepad with a clap of his hands. Johan was about to fall off his armchair.

'Well, I'm going to be honest with you,' the inspector adopted an almost friendly tone, which became increasingly harder. 'The police always catch the people who are guilty of crimes. Do you know what the only difference is? That the longer you take to confess, the more time I will have wasted and the bigger my anger will be. However, if we solve this here, in this room, between all of us, I will be generous. After all it's Christmas, isn't it? If I leave this house with the idol under my arm and Mr Crispin recovers from the shock, it will all have been just a bad joke.'

Appleby watched the reactions that his short speech had provoked. His audience seemed to be formed by a collection of statues. Even Miss Marsh had stopped wringing her hands. They didn't even blink. Since everybody remained silent, he continued.

'Well. I'll try to make myself clearer. In the three hours that I've spent here I've obtained at least one confession and evidence that incriminates more than one person.'

It was a lie, but Appleby threw the bait to see if anyone swallowed it. The amount of nervousness in his audience had certainly increased, especially in Johan, Clifford and Miss Marsh. James, Dickson, Mrs Sayers and Marie looked at the others, as if they expected some imminent confession. Nemo was still absorbed, looking at the miniature Roman boat.

The inspector cleared his throat, a bit uncomfortable.

'All right. I'll help you a little bit,' Appleby made a gesture to Sergeant Carrados, who put a handkerchief on a Chinese table, for everyone to see. It had an object wrapped in it. 'Does this tell you anything?'

They all stretched their necks to examine it better. Nemo stopped looking at the miniature boat. Sergeant Carrados untied the corners of the handkerchief and showed its contents: three earthy stones and two wads of banknotes. They watched all that without saying a word, and without understanding anything, as if it were the first time they saw money or a handful of stones. The inspector gave a meaningful look to Nemo, who went pale.

'They were...' his voice failed him at first and he had to breathe deeply before he continued, 'they were the objects that I found in my pockets when I regained my consciousness.'

Everyone's looks turned to him. Clifford laughed dryly.

'I'm sorry, Nemo, but I always had a bad feeling about you.'

Appleby wasn't laughing at all. He looked as serious as if he were at a funeral.

'Young man, in case you're still having problems with your memory, let me remind you that it's getting late for me to go to the theatre. We have found those horrible looking stones in your room and they look amazingly similar to the stolen idol. They were well hidden at the bottom of an urn and well accompanied: they were together with one hundred pounds. How funny, during the interrogation you forgot to mention them. You're the only one without an alibi: you were alone when all the mess started. When I went into the library I caught you manipulating some of the evidence. However, I don't think you have been able to do it without any help. As Mrs Sayers, Miss Marsh and Mr Dickson are beyond any suspicion, it had to be one of these young people. So please, tell me who your accomplices are and let me get to the theatre on time.'

Nemo knew he was in big trouble. A sharp pain crossed him from the back of his neck. He was incapable of thinking. He had a mental block. James took a step forward to help him in his defence.

'With all due respect, Inspector, your accusation is quite... absurd. Nemo was one of the people who knocked the door down. He came into the library with us.'

'Can't you see it, James?' Clifford jumped. 'That was afterwards. He could have climbed to the roof, taken advantage of the distraction of the giant policeman and done something to the window.

O'Connor seemed to wake up from his lethargy.

'Do what, you silly thing?' James replied. 'Fly?'

'He could have hung from the roof with a string while this one was staring into space,' he pointed at O'Connor. 'You saw how he fell asleep when he was supposed to keep an eye on us.'

O'Connor jumped:

'Staring into space...? Do you want me to pull off your head?!'

He seemed ready to fulfil his threat, but Appleby stopped him just in time, with an impatient gesture of his hand.

'How did he get through the window bars?' Marie stood up next to where James was. 'Nemo is skinny, but not that much.'

'He may have sawed the bars off.'

James turned to Appleby:

'I'm sure they have already checked that.'

'Of course we have,' the inspector added. 'The bars are intact and in their place.'

'Besides he would need to be some sort of a superman,' Marie added. 'He hung off the roof, attacked Mr Crispin, went out of the room again, leapt back onto the roof and came running to the library door in... twenty seconds?'

'And after hearing the gunshot, I'm sure O'Connor had his eyes fixed on the window,' James concluded. 'He asked us from the garden what had happened. He was paying attention. He would have seen him come out.'

Clifford obstinately looked at them, with a stubborn expression and his fists clenched.

'I don't care! He's got the stones and the money. I think that's evidence.'

'It's really good evidence,' Appleby nodded, while he watched the time with a sombre expression. 'There have been people who have been sentenced to death with less evidence.' He turned to Nemo. 'The ball's in your court, Mr Amnesia. It's your turn to remember. Where have the stones come from and who gave you the money?'

'I've already answered that.'

'No, you haven't. Look, I don't know how many minor thefts you have taken part in, but I have witnessed at least a hundred times as many. And I will tell you that they all end in the same way. Always. Nobody knows anything, they never remember why the money was at the bottom of their wardrobe, or why the blood-stained knife was inside the marmalade jar... Until we gather the evidence. After the judge pronounces his verdict, then they do know, they suddenly remember. But then it's too late. I am offering you the possibility to confess your crime before it's too late for you. Now. Tell me where the idol is and who your accomplices are!'

Appleby had taken off his friendly mask. He tried to crush Nemo with a firey stare. The young man stood his ground. His head was spinning and his legs were trembling. The inspector shrugged his shoulders. He looked at Nemo with a scornful expression.

'Whatever you like, you'll have plenty of time to repent,' He turned to Sergeant Carrados. 'We have finished for today. Handcuff him and take him to the police station. To the rest of you, merry Christmas.'

Nemo suffered an attack of vertigo. It was obvious that the inspector hadn't found anything out during the interrogations. He wasn't going to admit his failure in front of his superiors either. The stones and the money were enough for him to save his face. He already had his scapegoat! Nemo couldn't let Appleby leave Crispin's mansion. He had to improvise something. Fast, now. Whatever it was. All the evidence was still fresh. As soon as the police left the house, the thief would make sure to eliminate every single piece of evidence that could incriminate him or her, and would take the idol out of there. If the Purple Rock disappeared, Nemo would waste the best years of his life inside the walls of a prison.

He felt a shiver as he was being handcuffed. He noticed Marie's sad expression. And Clifford's scornful look. Appleby was picking up his coat, and about to leave.

His fear wasn't letting him think clearly. And his head... the beating pain that started at the scar had assaulted his mind and crushed each and every one of this thoughts. He couldn't do anything. He felt an uncontrollable urge to cry.

Chapter seven

In check

Carrados pushed him so that he would move forward, Nemo stumbled and fell on his knees. His eyes were in front of one of the glass cabinets, at the level of the miniature Roman boat. A while ago he had been contemplating it, without knowing why. The light from the fireplace illumined its sails, as if it wanted to burn them. And then he saw it. Marie had said it: *One of the boats that Archimedes set on fire*. The flash of this revelation completely neutralised the pain in his head. An infinity of details that he had been observing in the last few hours fitted like pieces of a gear wheel mechanism, and finally made the machinery of his intelligence work. It happened the same way in which he had known that Marie was Polish or that Clifford spent his life stuck to the ocular of a microscope.

'Sir, there's a detail that you have forgotten about,' he said, almost out of breath.

Appleby was already at the door.

'I doubt it.' He winked at him and disappeared.

'The Purple Rock...'

His words were suspended in the air. One second after, the inspector's head reappeared at the threshold.

'Excuse me? I haven't heard you well.'

Nemo stood up clumsily, with Marie and James's help.

'You're leaving without the stolen object,' he answered. 'If you find theatre so boring, you're going to play a pathetic role in front of your superiors.'

'You've got an accomplice...' Appleby watched Nemo distrustfully. He threw his coat on a sofa and stood in front of the young man, with his hands on his hips, shaking his head. 'Children... I never seem to learn the lesson. All right, Captain Nemo. I'm going to give you fifteen seconds. If what you tell me is interesting enough, I will give you fifteen more... and so on. The moment I find it boring, I'll be leaving.'

Nemo swallowed hard. It was a very tight margin, but it had to be enough. It was either that or spending his life in prison.

'All right. It's a deal.'

'Well, you're wasting your time,' Appleby warned him, checking his pocket watch: 'you've already lost five seconds.'

'I don't even need the other ten: I know who committed the robbery.'

'Give me names.'

Nemo doubted for just one second. People say that before we die we see our whole lives in an instant. The life that Nemo could remember was just a few hours long. His mind revised the events that had led him to Mr Crispin's mansion. He heard Appleby impatiently clearing his throat and decided to trust his own instinct. With a dramatic gesture that the inspector considered a bad imitation of his own, he turned to Clifford, Johan, Marie and James.

'It was them, sir. The four of them.'

Clifford gave a scornful neigh. Johan's cheeks turned whiter than porcelain cups. James and Marie exchanged looks. In their expression the same reproach could be read: "How can he be so ungrateful."

Appleby stopped their complaints by clapping his hands.

'Shhhh. Quiet everybody. Everybody except you, Captain Nemo. Fifteen seconds…'

'I also know where the idol is.'

'Don't play with my hopes any longer, Nemo. Where?'

'Do you fancy a glass of brandy?'

'I never drink when I'm on duty. And to tell the truth, I don't drink the rest of the time, either. I prefer celery juice.'

Nemo wrinkled his nose.

'You don't even need to drink a drop of brandy. The only thing you need to do is look at the bottle top.'

Appleby's hunting instinct was awakened.

'Where is it?' he asked with a very thin voice.

'I've no idea,' Nemo shrugged his shoulders, 'Mr Trent took it. Could it be in the kitchen?'

Appleby asked Trent, who pointed at Miss Marsh with his head… and she stuttered her answer:

'It's… I le-left it in the kitchen pantry.'

Appleby sent Carrados to look for it. The next two minutes became eternal. Nemo's ears were ringing with atrocious intensity. He didn't know if it was because of the wound or because of what Marie, Clifford, James and Johan must be thinking about him. At last, Carrados reappeared with a fat orange bottle. The inspector jumped as if he had been propelled by a spring, took the bottle off his hands and opened it.

'This bottle top looks absolutely...' He was going to say "ordinary", but the fact that it moved when he pushed it with his fingers, wasn't ordinary at all. From inside it, he extracted a dark, mineral object. 'Is this little piece of... rubbish...?'

Nemo nodded.

'It's Nacthali's heart, sir. If you don't like it, neither do I.'

'It doesn't matter whether we like it or not, does it?' Appleby had an ear-to-ear grin. 'So you hid it here, you rascal... Very ingenious.'

'I didn't hide it, sir.'

'Of course, sorry. I was forgetting the fact that you are innocent. So, how did you know it was there?'

'I have deduced it. I'm surprised that you're surprised. Isn't your job precisely about deducing things that people don't know or don't tell you?'

Appleby was affected by the blow, and a little offended:

'I am the only here who has the right to be sarcastic. And I am also the only one who can ask questions: How did you know that the idol was in the bottle top?'

Nemo scratched his head.

'I'm going to need a little more than fifteen seconds to answer that.'

The inspector showed him his open hand and shook his five fingers in front of him.

'I'm extending your time limit to five minutes.'

And he sat down, pretending to be annoyed. In fact, he was radiantly happy. He had just recovered the stolen object. He intended to take all the praise for it without attributing any merit to Nemo. The young man also experimented a profound relief. He breathed deeply. The possibility of going to prison seemed to be more distant now. Instead of feeling fear, there was a new type of feeling coming over him. An impulsive and consuming rage. Rage against those who had put him in that horrendous situation. Rage against those who had been about to ruin his life. Rage against whoever had stolen his memories. Now it was time for him to take revenge.

'I knew where the idol was from the very beginning,' he stated. 'There weren't that many options. It was inside the library before we entered and it wasn't there when they searched us. Someone must have taken it out before. Owing to the precautions that Mr Trent quickly adopted, there were only three people or things, as far as I know, that went out of the room. Mr Crispin, Trent himself and the bottle that Johan passed on to the detective. I can't doubt Trent's honourableness, nor his professional behaviour when he searched Mr Crispin. If the idol had been in the brandy, they would have found it when they served him a drink. So the only possibility left was the bottle top.

Appleby felt for his notepad with his notes, in a jacket pocket. Why hadn't he thought of something so obvious? To avoid looking embarrassed, he gave Johan his hawk stare. He was trembling like a medium about to speak the words of a hundred different spirits.

'I told you that all of them took part in it,' he continued. 'Johan took the idol out, but it was the only thing he did.'

'It's no little thing. And what did the others do?'

'I will start from the beginning: Nachtali's supernatural visit. When it was twelve o'clock, a bell could be heard ringing. Dickson, who was at the entrance hall, went in response to the call, but he went in the wrong direction.'

'What do you mean in the wrong direction?' Dickson combed his eyebrows with two trembling fingers. 'It's not true, sir. I went to the door.'

'That's what I was saying: in the wrong direction. The same thing happened to me a while ago when I was in the greenhouse. I heard a noise and I thought that it was coming from somewhere in front of me, but it had been behind me. We trust our senses, but they blatantly lie to us. We only have two ears, and with the information they obtain, our brain has to locate any source of sound. How does it do it? Let's imagine a circle around your head,' Nemo drew it with his finger around him, 'and imagine we place doorbells along this circumference. In most cases, the bells will be nearer to one ear than to the other one. When the brain compares the intensity of the sound that each of the ears registers, it becomes disoriented. But what happens if the doorbell is situated at the same distance from both ears? The brain then gets the same information from both channels, and how will it tell whether the doorbell is in front of him or behind him?'

'By using the eyesight...,' Marie suggested.

'For instance. And what if nothing can be seen? It then solves the problem by following expectations. If your brain expects the doorbell to be in front of you, you will hear it in front of you. If it expects it to be behind you, you will hear it behind you. That's the way it works. Dickson was expecting someone to ring the bell. In front of him. Someone rang a bell behind him, making sure to do it at exactly the same distance from both his ears. And Dickson's brain decided to open the door. He didn't find anybody on the other side, of course. *Because there was nobody*. The bell he heard wasn't the doorbell, but one of the bells that was decorating the Christmas tree behind him, next to the staircase. That fir tree is so big that it was decorated with the same bells that are used to call the servants. And who fooled Dickson? The person who was with him then: our friend Clifford.'

'You're a disgrace!'

Clifford shouted angrily, but he had lost all the self-confidence that he used to show. After insulting Nemo, he was incapable of saying a single word more, which in his case seemed very revealing.

'How much time have I got left?' Nemo asked the inspector.

'You've got an open bar. As much time as you need, Captain,' Appleby answered him. 'Please continue…'

'Dickson is a very experienced man who fought in the Indian Mutiny, but he has a weak point: he believes in spirits. That put him in an impressionable state of mind. What happened at the door made him feel even more scared. When Clifford started to shout like a madman that he was feeling a ghostly presence and hearing its footsteps, that was what triggered Dickson's self-suggestion.'

'But I did hear the footsteps!' Dickson protested, with a growing sense of confusion.

'It's true, but they weren't the footsteps of an eskimo god going for a run. The footsteps came from upstairs. They were her footsteps,' Nemo pointed at Marie. 'Those huge boots with spikes make up for her light weight and they banged the floor like hammers. In his attempt to leave the house stained with pig's blood, Johan had made Miss Marsh furious. Dickson gave the order to remove the carpets from the corridor upstairs. I myself helped remove them and I can assure you that they weigh a ton. Dickson isn't used to hearing any footsteps upstairs, because there is usually an extremely thick carpet that muffles them. Marie's footsteps were a new element in a context of great nervousness, in which Clifford led him to thinking about a ghostly presence. To sum up, Clifford created the effect at the entrance, Marie was responsible for the supernatural footsteps and Johan took the idol out of the library.

'And me?' James asked in anticipation, with one of his charming smiles. 'What did I do?'

'You? I'm sorry to say that you did everything else, James. You planned the robbery and you tricked the others into it. Marie, Johan and Clifford didn't know what they were doing. Marie and Johan were absolutely innocent. Clifford was only half-innocent. This morning, before twelve o'clock, you told him that you had thought about a great idea to play a joke on Dickson and scare him to death, and of course, poor thing, he couldn't resist the temptation. You had been playing heavy jokes on him for days. Do you remember the pumpkin ectoplasm? When Clifford thought that a ghost had actually tried to kill Mr Crispin, he didn't find the joke that funny. It was making him become an accomplice of the robbery. That's why he has been so quiet since then.'

Clifford kept his eyes fixed on his baseball shoes. Appleby cleared his throat.

'Is all that he is saying true?'

'Yes, it is.'

He said it in an almost inaudible tone of voice, but in the expectant silence that had filled the room, everyone managed to hear his answer. The inspector rubbed his hands and sat comfortably in his armchair. He took the bottle of brandy and poured himself a glass.

'I'm going to make an exception, just for today,' he justified himself. Then he looked at Nemo with sincere appreciation. 'I won't deny that you're exposing some of the ideas that I had written down on my notepad,' He patted his jacket pocket. 'But let's continue. Where were we? How could anyone enter the library, shoot at Mr Crispin and vanish into thin air before you knocked the door down?'

'James shot the gun.'

The young mathematician laughed out loud.

'How could I do it? Going through the wall? Come on, Nemo. Five people saw me arrive to the library door: Trent, Marie, Clifford, Dickson, Johan... Do you need any more witnesses? We heard the gunshot when we were together.'

'That's true, Nemo,' Marie said, with a doubtful tone of voice.

'I know, Marie. I said that James shot the gun, not that he shot it when we thought we heard it. He shot the gun yesterday.'

'Yesterday. Yes, of course,' James nodded. 'And it made its sound one day after.'

'No, it made its sound yesterday.'

'And why didn't anyone hear it?'

'We all heard it, but we didn't know we were hearing a gunshot. You made sure to buy a box of *crackers* and then pass it to Clifford. What was the result of that? An afternoon in which we didn't stop hearing bursts,' Dickson, Mrs Sayers and Miss Marsh vehemently nodded in front of Appleby's inquisitive look. 'You created the perfect atmosphere for a gunshot to be heard without anybody paying any attention to it. Very bright.'

'But we heard a gunshot in the library today, and there was a cloud of smoke,' Marie objected.

'We all saw the gunpowder,' Nemo admitted, 'and, as we had heard a detonation and later found a bullet, we concluded that someone had shot a gun. But where was it? I found it difficult to understand the answer, even though it was obvious. *We didn't find any guns because there weren't any guns.* We didn't hear a gunshot, we heard an explosion, which is very different.'

Nemo took a pause and realised that the others were listening to every single word he said, as if their lives depended on them. The inspector sipped his glass of brandy and invited him to continue with a wide smile.

'You've got us on tenterhooks, Nemo. Who or what caused the explosion? Mr Crispin?' Nemo shook his head. 'A ghost then? There wasn't a clockwork mechanism in the library. Nobody could have taken it in or out of the library. The room was tightly closed and guarded by two policemen.'

'Not so well closed. There was a tiny hole through which someone could come in.'

'On the wall? On the ceiling? Under the door?' Appleby shook his head emphatically. My men have examined it all carefully. I can assure you they are very good. They can't have overlooked something like that.'

'Well they certainly have overlooked it. Have they noticed the little hole in the curtain?'

'You've gone too far with that one, Nemo,' James protested. 'Who would try to enter the library through that hole?'

Marie suddenly jumped up from her seat.

'The sunlight! The heat can provoke a detonation…'

'Exactly,' Nemo smiled for the first time for many hours. He turned to the inspector, who had got lost in the explanations. 'There is a hole in the library window's curtain, which lets in a ray of light. Mr Crispin uses it to reproduce Newton's experiment. The ray of light usually reaches the prism. But someone made a change there.' He turned to Johan and Marie. 'Do you remember who suggested pulling the curtain shut?'

'James…'

'Once the room was dark, he used the opportunity to change the prism for a looking glass. Did you notice the clothes peg? What was it doing the library? He used it to hold the looking glass upright. He moved away the screen on which the rainbow is usually projected and replaced it with an ashtray full of gunpowder. How much time did Nachtali give Crispin to return the Purple Rock? Until midday. Why did he choose such an inconvenient time for a ghost? Any astronomer, including James himself, could explain to you that it is at that time when the rays from the Sun reach the Earth with their highest intensity. Do you know Archimedes' story?'

Appleby nodded, in a not very convincing way.

'Of course. Who doesn't?'

'Archimedes burnt the Roman boats besieging the city of Syracuse. He did it from some distance, from the city walls, by concentrating the heat from the sun rays on the sails, using mirrors. James carried out a more modest version of the experiment. The looking glass in the library concentrated the ray of sunlight that was filtered through the curtain on a point of the ashtray, while Crispin was reading in his armchair. When the gunpowder reached its igniting temperature, it provoked the explosion that broke the ashtray.'

'Gunpowder burns, but it doesn't explode, unless it is confined in a very limited space,' Marie interrupted him, while she thought, 'He must have mixed it with another ingredient. Where could he have taken it from? Ah, from the *crackers*! For them to crack, they've got inside a string impregnated in silver fulminate. It's an explosive component that is extremely sensitive to rubbing or heat.'

'Thank you, Marie. We'll analyse the fragments from the ashtray in the laboratory,' Appleby said. 'Well, Nemo. This investigation is on fire, in more than one sense...'

'When we knocked the door down, we were under some strong self-suggestion. Something supernatural had just happened. As soon as we found Mr Crispin lying on the floor, with his shirt stained with blood and mumbling, all our attention was focused on him. James knew that he had at least one minute's margin to do anything he needed without anyone noticing him. He used his time well. He changed the looking glass for the prism again. He took the idol from the table and put it inside an empty cork bottle top. He exchanged the bottle tops and finally pulled the curtain open. However, as he had so little time, I doubt that he wasted it deleting his own fingerprints. The ones on the bottle top seem particularly compromising to me.'

'But it was not him who took the idol out of the room.'

'No, it was Johan. You need to understand, Inspector, that James is a master of improvisation. He would have taken care of it personally if he hadn't had a choice, but he preferred to let someone else do it so as not to attract too much to attention to himself,' Nemo turned to Johan. 'Why did you take the bottle? It's one of the few initiatives that I've seen you take since I met you.'

'When Trent was going to take Crispin out, James said that a glass of brandy would do him good to revive him,' Johan answered, about to pull another button off his jacket. 'I was next to the cocktail cabinet. He gestured to me to do it and that's why I took the bottle.'

Nemo gave Appleby an eloquent gesture:

'So James only had to wait until you went to the theatre to go to the kitchen and take the fake bottle top with the Purple Rock.'

'We still have Mr Crispin's shouts, his desperate request for help, the bloodstain on his shirt...'

'You described his state with absolute precision when you came here: he was suffering from hallucinatory delirium, induced by an alkaloid. Did you notice his widened pupils? I don't know the method that James used. I'm not an expert on hallucinogens. Maybe they can be poured in a drink.'

'They certainly can,' Appleby nodded. 'Thorndyke's report will clarify things for us.'

'And the stain on the shirt, is not a bloodstain, it's red ink. They sell it at any shop in the Chinese quarter as a joking item. It's an invisible ink that becomes red with the heat of the body. They call it the "vampire's sweat".'

'What fun. Another job for the laboratory,' Appleby nodded, 'Is there anything else that we are forgetting?'

'There's no need to say that James didn't see any eskimo from the second floor window.'

'I understand,' Appleby scratched his chin while he mentally revised what Nemo had told him. 'And what if it had been a cloudy day.'

Nemo shrugged his shoulders.

'He wouldn't have tried the robbery. And the same thing would have happened if Dickson had realised that Clifford was fooling him. Or that the supernatural steps were caused by Marie's boots... James prepared a collection of tricks, and he could step out of the game whenever he wanted. Nothing would compromise him until the end. The only irreversible step was the robbery itself, which he left for the last minute. Dickson swallowed the bait, it was sunny enough, the detonation took place, the supernatural effect worked perfectly well, the alkaloid did its effect exactly when it was supposed to. So he continued...'

'Wasn't there an easier way to do it?'

'Nachtali's warning served as an excuse for Crispin to take his extremely expensive meteorite out of its armoured chamber and placed it in a vulnerable position. The paranormal show distracted everyone's attention. Think about it. If you hadn't found the stones and the money, what would you have now? A robbery that would be both absurd and uncomfortable. You might end up archiving it in the folder where you keep all the unexplainable cases.'

'There is no such folder in Scotland Yard,' Appleby replied decidedly. 'And now that you've mentioned the stones and the money...'

'I told you the truth. I can't remember who I am nor how they ended up in my pocket. But I can make some guesses. I don't know if you have noticed that James has stood up in my defence.'

'Yes, I must admit that's something that I find difficult to understand.'

'You asked me a minute ago: "Wasn't there an easier way to steal the idol?". Of course there was. There was an alternative plan, but it didn't work. Doctor Thorndyke told me that I could recover my memory at any moment. No, James wasn't interested in me going to prison, remembering everything all of a sudden, and exposing him when I felt betrayed. He was interested in making sure that the hypothesis of an unexplainable robbery was chosen.'

'So you think that you knew each other before?'

'When we left Mr Crispin in the library, someone blew out Johan's candle. James asked us if we had a light, and when I took my hands to my pockets, what a coincidence, I found the piece of paper that Mr Carrados took away from me when they searched me. I am convinced that a graphological analysis will certify that it was written by James.'

Appleby nodded. He could perfectly remember the anonymous note with the appointment for Nemo to go to the greenhouse.

'He wanted you to be away. I'm not surprised. I wouldn't want to have you near me if I were trying to steal something.'

Nemo took it as a compliment and smiled.

'He had devised another plan to steal the idol from the armoured chamber, for which he needed an accomplice. He sent me the one hundred pounds and the three stones. The money was sent to try to tempt me. I don't know what my situation was when I arrived to London. I was probably in trouble. The stones are meteorites and he gave them to me so that I could recognise the Purple Rock. We must have arranged to meet in the alley. I want to believe that I rejected his offer. Perhaps I threatened to report him to the police if he carried on with his plan. We fought and he hit me. Did he think he had killed me? Maybe someone came closer when hearing the argument and forced him to run away? When he saw me in the mansion, he reacted with an expression of terror. I felt surprised then, but I was so numb from the commotion that I didn't pay attention to that. The true thing is James wasn't comfortable at all until Clifford told him that I had lost my memory.'

Inspector Appleby sat back in his armchair, absent-mindedly, and finished up his glass of brandy.

'The story seems too good to be true,' he said before turning to James. 'What do you think?'

As Nemo explained his theory, James had been losing his expressiveness. He had the same face, but somehow he had become a different person. He was now standing, with his hands in his pockets, looking indifferent, as if they weren't talking about him. Before answering Appleby, he slowly smiled.

'It's true that I did arrange with Clifford a joke to be played on Dickson,' he shrugged his shoulders. 'It's nothing personal, but the situation was clearly asking for it. About the rest... I can only tell you that I saw an eskimo from the window. If you believe something different, then prove it.'

Appleby nodded.

'I don't think it will require too much work. Captain Nemo has told us very clearly what needs to be done: graphological, chemical, fingerprint and drug intake analyses... The result of these tests will definitely tell us what we need to know, but do you know what the most convincing detail is to me? Nemo couldn't know it, but when he checked you, Sergeant Carrados found a brandy bottle top in your waistcoat pocket. We didn't consider it very important then. Now, of course, I see it differently,' he turned to Carrados,

'That's all right. We're changing our plan and our prisoner. We're talking young James... what was your surname?'

'Moriarty, sir,' James answered proudly.

'Young James Moriarty...' Appleby sighed and checked his watch one more time. It was seven o'clock. If he hurried up, he was still in time to sleep through the second act.

Carrados freed Nemo from his handcuffs, which changed the pair of hands they were holding when James was handcuffed.

The young man kept his smile in spite of the fact that everything looked bad for him. His eyes, however, didn't smile. Marie couldn't help shivering.

While he rubbed his wrists, Nemo approached Appleby, who was picking up his coat for the last time.

'Can I ask you a favour?'

'Go ahead. But don't take too long.'

Nemo then turned to James.

'Who am I? You know it...'

In fact, it wasn't a question, but a command. James's terrible smile became more intense. His voice, however, sounded calm, almost placid:

'Who knows? Aren't you that intelligent? I don't want to spoil your amusement. Think, and I'm sure you will find out.'

In his eyes there was a hard stare that seemed to cut like a knife. Nemo lowered his head. His look of disappointment was the only thing that James could take with him to prison. The only thing that, after all, he had been able to steal from Mr Crispin's mansion.

Epilogue

In clear

Cyril Appleby arrived just in time to fall asleep for the second act of the *The Hunchbacked Man's Slippers*. The morning after he started a methodical investigation, which confirmed Nemo's deductions bit by bit. He also clarified certain details that they hadn't been able to clarify yet, for instance, the motive for the robbery. James's father, Jerrold Moriarty, was an illustrious lawyer who had gone bankrupt because of some risky financial speculation. The servants who worked for Nigel Ackroyd, the collector who had lost the bid for the Purple Rock, admitted that their master had been seen meeting with James a couple of times. The young man never admitted the fact that he was guilty. Once recovered from the scare and the hallucinogens, Mr Crispin didn't want to present charges against him, but the machinery of the justice system had already started to work. James Moriarty was sentenced to one year in prison. In the Newgate prison he made some friends with questionable behaviour, who taught him a thousand ways to pay for his studies without having to ask his family for help. His book *The*

Dynamics of an Asteroid is still very highly considered among the classic works of modern astronomy. Unfortunately, with the passing of time, some other more mundane activities distracted him from his interest in science.

Appleby let Nemo look at the register of missing people that Scotland Yard kept. They both went through the lists of passengers on all the boats that had arrived to English ports in the week before he had come into Mr Crispin's house. Not a single name led the young man to remembering anything. Appleby was assigned the position of Chief Inspector that he had been eagerly waiting for, and he asked Nemo to work with him in a new division for criminal investigation. The young man was thankful for the offer, but before making a decision, he needed to clarify his ideas.

Mr Crispin was so grateful to Nemo that he even offered to adopt him. The young man simply accepted his hospitality. Three days after Nachtali's attack, Clifford, Johan and Marie packed their luggage to return to their homes. Clifford was about to suffer a spontaneous combustion when Gideon declared the prize void. The jury of the competition, formed by five distinguished members of London's Royal Society, had voted for James Moriarty. Gideon refused to give him a single penny from his money. However, he realised that if he had presented the best investigation project, he couldn't give the prize to someone else.

Nemo only said goodbye to Marie. He went with her to Victoria Station and stayed there, waiting at the platform, while the porters pushed the luggage trolleys in a rush. Marie, who had already made herself comfortable in her compartment, slid the glass window down and stooped to look out, and have one last conversation with Nemo.

'I don't know how many friends you had in the past, but from now on you can count on at least one. You can count on me.'

'Thank you, Marie. I'm sure you're worth as much as all the friends I have forgotten about. Your only defect is that you're Polish and you need to go back to Poland.'

'You've got your home there. I'll write to you, to Mr Crispin's address. For the moment, the recipient will be Captain Nemo. In a few weeks' time you will tell me what your real name is.'

Nemo was deeply thankful of the fact that she took for granted that he was going to find out what his real name was. A bell rang at the station. The ticket collector stopped checking the carriages to make sure that all the doors were closed. The engine's whistle was heard, out of tune, and a long plume of smoke came out from the chimney.

'Goodbye, Marie. Don't stop investigating!'

'Of course I won't.'

'If you have no other choice, you should marry a chemist.'

Marie winked at him:

'Oh yes, and if possible, one who is handsome and has his own laboratory.'

'Of course. There must be someone like that. Even if you have to travel to Paris to find him. I mean it. Don't waste your talent. Show the Cliffords and Jameses of the world how good you are.'

The screeching of the wheels on the rails didn't let him understand Marie's last words. The train left the station. Standing at one end of the platform, Nemo waved his hand, while Marie did the same, leaning out of the window, until she became so tiny in the distance that he was incapable of distinguishing her face. He had the feeling that his only friend was leaving. A huge loss in his extremely brief history.

Doctor Thorndyke had told him that the normal thing would be for his amnesia to start to diminish in the first few weeks. After one month and a half, Nemo lost all hope of recovering his memory. But even so, he still couldn't give up on it. He could constantly hear James's last words in his mind: "Aren't you that intelligent? Think, and I'm sure you will find out." Nemo's accent was from London. Someone must know him there. He bought a map and methodically visited every single shop. He could be seen in every square, every market, every train station. He looked at everyone's eyes to check their reactions, hoping to find in them a spark that indicated that they had recognised him. Most people looked away. A few looked at him suspiciously or defiantly.

As weeks passed by, his hopes started to fade. In his map, all the streets in the centre had been crossed out. He went on with his search in the outskirts, out of pure stubbornness. There were only a couple of districts left for him to visit.

That was how he found Deptford, a neighbourhood in Southeast London. When St. Paul' clock struck half past seven, he decided that the little shop that he could see across the street, selling fine art materials, was going to be his last try of the day. Mr Crispin would be waiting to have lunch with him in one hour's time. He had spent the whole afternoon going in and out of about thirty shops, unsuccessfully, and he was tired. It was already dark and London showed its least welcoming appearance. The yellowish light from the lampposts could hardly make its way through the thick fog. Nemo saw the city as an animal that has been beaten by the cold winter weather. He took comfort in the thought of Mrs Sayers's pudding. It was still half an hour before the closing time of the shops, and people in the street were rushing back home, holding onto their hats to make sure they weren't blown away by the wind.

In the shop window, the paintbrushes were covered in dust and cobwebs, and they were surrounded by painter's easels and canvases placed without any apparent order. Nemo thought he recognised a couple of the paintings, but didn't have high hopes about them. He had had similar delusions many times before. The door was half-open.

There was nobody at the counter. Soon after the brass cowbell that was hanging from the door frame rang, some shuffling footsteps coming from the back room could be heard. From a narrow aisle a woman came out. She was wiping her paint-stained hands on her apron. She had a smell of linseed oil and turpentine that seemed familiar and made him feel comfortable. Nemo watched her face closely and he immediately felt a strong disappointment. Her face didn't look at all familiar. She smiled when she saw him.

'I thought you were in Paris. When did you come back?'

Nemo's heartbeat stopped for a second and then re-started, out of control.

'Do you know... who I am?' he asked with a hoarse voice that seemed about to break.

The woman laughed, unable to understand.

'What do you mean if I know who you are? It hasn't been so long that I can't remember you. After all, what has it been? Seven months?'

Nemo had to lean on the counter. His legs were shaking so heavily that he could hardly stand. He tried to smile back, with a mixture of friendliness and helplessness, which touched the woman's feelings very deeply.

'If I ask you a question, will you answer me?'

'Of course. That is, if I know the answer and it hasn't got anything to do with my age...'

'What's my name?'

The woman slightly opened her lips, looking puzzled, and the young man was breathless. The strong feelings were about to overwhelm him.

'What's happened to you?' The shopkeeper's face looked worried. 'Are you all right?'

But the young man didn't answer. Tears were about to fall from his wide open eyes. He remained attentive, obstinately waiting for an answer.

'Holmes, Sherlock Holmes...' the woman said at last, almost indignantly. 'That has always been your name. At least, ever since your parents took you to be baptised at St. Chad's parish church in Yorkshire.'

'Sherlock?' Nemo asked, surprised.

Sherlock Holmes? His first impression was that it was a bit of an eccentric name. As he started to repeat it to himself, as if it were a mantra, he felt as if a huge weight was being lifted off him.

He spent the rest of the afternoon in the shop, learning many things about himself that he had forgotten. When he came out into the street again, the cold weather and the darkness that the lampposts could barely fight against, were no longer able to make him feel discouraged. The wound was completely healed. He helped the woman, Mrs Phyllis James, to cover the shop window with planks. She later took care of locking the shop and gave him a piece of paper where he had written the address of his older brother, Mycroft Holmes. Sherlock thanked her for everything and sealed her forehead with a loud kiss. Then he ran to Mr Crispin's mansion to inform him about his real name. And to excuse himself, because that night they weren't going to share Mrs Sayers's exquisite pudding. That night he preferred to sleep at home.

APPENDIX

But, who on earth would think of something like that?

Marie Curie

Marie Curie's life could be told as a horror story. However, in spite of the fact that she was scared thousands of times, she never screamed or ran away. Marie was born in Warsaw, in 1867. She was born in a beautiful place, but at a time that was not beautiful at all. Austria, Prussia

and Russia had decided to divide Poland between them as if it were a birthday cake. Marie's family had to live in the Russian portion. At school, the lessons were in Russian, but the Polish people around her taught her the language and history of her country secretly, so Marie had to study double! Besides, her parents were both teachers. From the moment when she woke up until she went to bed, wherever she was, she was always with a teacher. Terrifying, isn't it?

As this is a horror story, it's time to mention the scariest moments. When Marie was ten years old, her older sister died of typhus. Two years later, her mother died of tuberculosis.

Marie completed her secondary education with the best marks in her class, although she was two years younger than her classmates. She had been born with an extraordinary brain and she loved learning, so she was going to have a wonderful time at university, wasn't she? Well, she wasn't. From then on, her life turned into a zombie film. Marie was surrounded by people who looked normal, but as soon as they heard her say that she wanted to be a chemist, or a physicist or a mathematician, they rolled their eyes, their nose bled, they broke dishes or had foam coming out of their mouths.

In Poland, like in most countries in the world, women were not allowed to study a degree course during that period. Luckily, there were also little strongholds that were free from zombies. One of them was in Paris. Marie and her sister Bronia soon devised a plan to escape from the living dead. Marie would work as a governess to pay for Bronia's studies of Medicine. When she graduated, they would exchange roles, and it would be her sister who would support her.

Although there were less zombies in Paris, life there was still scary for her. She rented a tiny attic in the Latin Quarter, which was a sixth floor without a lift. When she went out into the street and realised it was raining, she never returned for her umbrella even if it was pouring. Someone had lent her a little heater to keep herself warm, but as she didn't have a cent to even buy the coal to burn in it, most of the time it was as cold as the rest of the house. In winter nights the water in her washbasin turned into a block of ice. In order not to end up like a frozen pizza, Marie piled up all her clothes (which weren't that many) on top of her bed before going to sleep.

The world that surrounded her might have been depressing, but when Marie started to think about things related to science, everything else around her disappeared. She even forgot to eat. To tell the truth, when she did remember to eat, she didn't have much food anyway. With her little money she was barely able to buy a little chocolate and bread and a few fruits and eggs. One day she even fainted from hunger in the street.

If you are afraid of mathematics or physics, this is the point when the story becomes really scary, because what Marie did in that frozen and miserable attic, in which she was feeling terribly hungry, was… solve extremely difficult equations and plan all sorts of experiments. In Physics, she graduated as the top student of her class, and in Mathematics, she was the second student. When the zombies found out, they rolled their eyes, had foam coming out of their mouths and broke lots of dishes. Marie smiled.

After studying so much, and feeling so cold and hungry, she reached the conclusion that she had to start her professional career in Chemistry. She needed a laboratory desperately! A physicist friend of hers, introduced him to another physicist, Pierre Curie, head of the laboratory at the Municipal School for Industrial Physics and Chemistry of Paris. Marie asked him if he could make some room for her among his test tubes. Pierre gladly accepted the request, fell in love with her and asked her if she could make some room for him in her life. Marie couldn't say no: Pierre too forgot to eat when he was thinking about scientific projects! They had very romantic conversations about magnetism or the effect of electricity on glass. Their hearts beat faster. Everyone else ran away from them. Marie's wedding dress was a dark blue work outfit, which she would later find very useful at the laboratory.

By that time, there was something very disturbing taking place deep inside atoms. When the old photographic plates were exposed to sunlight, they became darker. A French physicist, Henri Becquerel, had discovered that uranium stones had the same property, even though they weren't bright. Those stones behaved like tiny dark-coloured suns that fogged the photographic plates in the dark. How could they do it? There must be some invisible rays coming out from uranium, which were even more penetrating than light itself, because they could even go through opaque objects. What were they made of? Nobody knew.

The uranic rays seemed intriguing and scary. They were the perfect subject for Marie's investigation. At the end of the 19th century there were about seventy chemical elements known. Marie experimented with as many as he could, even if they were difficult to pronounce, such as strontium and molybdenum. She wanted to know if any of them emitted uranic rays. He could only detect them in thorium. Uranium and thorium were the first radioactive elements known. Marie gave them that name because the word "ray" comes from the Latin word *radius*.

Chemical elements are like the ingredients that are used to cook, in the sense that they are rarely found alone, and when they are mixed, the results obtained can be very different. Salt tastes very good on chips, but it tastes horrible when it's added to a strawberry yogurt. Likewise, carbon combined with oxygen produces a gas and when you add hydrogen to it you have wood or sugar. The differences are because of the way in which the atoms are combined. However, Marie discovered that the mysterious rays didn't depend on these combinations. It didn't matter if uranium was isolated, as a metal, or if it was associated with oxygen to create minerals: it was still radioactive. She came to the conclusion that the rays came from the heart of the element itself.

As she learned more about this mystery, she found out more disturbing things. Pitchblende, a mineral from uranium emitted even stronger rays than pure uranium. How could this be possible? Marie suspected that inside pitchblende there was an unknown element, much more dreadful than uranium and thorium. Instead of running away, she decided to unmask it.

You may imagine chemists wearing white coats, working in a bright space, full of shiny glass tubes and bottles. Marie's laboratory was an old dissection room and in it, she looked like a witch preparing potions in her cauldron. In the pitchblende mineral there was not only uranium and a hidden secret element. We could almost say that there was nearly everything: iron, aluminium, lead, silicon... There were even pine needles in it!

Bracing herself with patience, Marie tried all methods of chemical decomposition on pitchblende. Little by little, she separated the atoms of known elements from the mixture, which progressively led her to having purer samples of the mysterious element. It was really hard work, but it was worth her effort. In the end there wasn't one hidden element only, there were two! To annoy Russians, Austrians and Prussians a little bit, she called the first one polonium. The second one, the most powerful one in the series, even more terrifying than uranium, thorium and polonium, she called radium.

After three years of great effort, from 1 000 000 g of pitchblende, Marie managed to extract 0.1 g of radium chloride (a combination of chlorine and radium). The little

Marie Curie in her laboratory.

white stone that she obtained seemed magical. It behaved like a miniature sun. When you took it heated up your hand without burning, and it shone in the dark, with a spectral bluish brightness. It burnt paper, altered the colour of glasses and the chemical composition of air, which smelled of ozone and was able to conduct electricity. The samples of radium turned Pierre and Marie's laboratory into a room full of ghosts. This is how she described it: "One of our greatest joys was to go into our workroom at night; we then perceived on all sides the feebly luminous silhouettes of the bottles of capsules containing our products. It was really a lovely sight and one always new to us. The glowing tubes looked like faint, fairy lights." Lovely? Would you dare to spend a night at the Curies' laboratory? Brrr.

At this point, things were going too well for the Curies. When you watch a horror film, you know that ten minutes after the last scare, you're approaching another one that will leave you stuck to your seat. That's what happened in Marie's life. One spring afternoon, while Pierre went for a walk thinking about scientific matters, the world around him disappeared. That's why he couldn't see a horse carriage that was coming towards him. He was run over, and died instantly.

It was an extremely hard blow for Marie. Now that Pierre wasn't there anymore, she felt very lonely and missed having someone to talk to about hidden elements or lethal rays, while she had breakfast or went for a walk. She took comfort in talking to her daughters. The eldest liked it so much, that she decided to become a chemist herself. It was her who discovered artificial radioactivity and produced combinations of chemical elements that didn't exist in nature and that emitted uranic rays.

Have you ever heard that a person "died of success"? That's literally what happened to Marie. She reached scientific glory thanks to her discovery of radium, but the mysterious rays gravely damaged the cells in her body. There are some people who need to sleep hugging a teddy bear. Marie preferred to leave a radioactive mineral on her bedside table. She was so fascinated by the new element that she played at all times with it. She wrote, for example, that "if a radioactive substance is placed in the dark near the eye or the temples, a sensation of light fills the eye." The long exposure to radioactivity made Marie get ill and ended up killing her. The notebooks from her laboratory are so terrible and dangerous that reading them could kill you. But it's not because of a curse. They were written in the ghostly laboratory that shone in the dark and their pages were impregnated with radioactivity. Today they are kept in a lead-lined box.

Marie was the first woman to do many things. She was the first one to be awarded a doctorate in France, for example, to teach at the Sorbonne University in Paris or to receive a Nobel prize. Many men used to think that studying hurt women, both physically and mentally. With Marie's achievements, they didn't have arguments. She proved that when a woman likes science, the best thing one can do is to let her investigate in peace.

The terrible rays

What were those mysterious rays that came out of uranium, radium and polonium minerals? Marie was right to suppose that they came from the heart of atoms themselves. In fact, the personality of each chemical element is inside the nucleus of its atoms. Do you want sodium? Well, you need to gather eleven protons. Do you want gold? Gather seventy-nine protons. Don't forget to add some neutrons to the mixture, to make it stick together well, because protons are a little contradictory. They partially

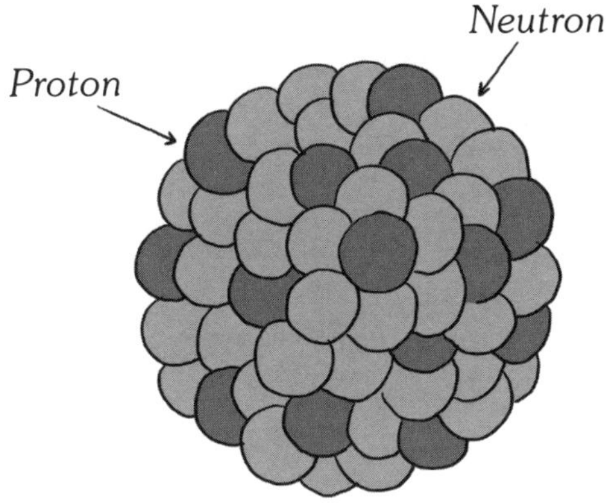

Portrait of an atomic nucleus, with all its neutrons and protons.

attract each other, but partially repel each other too. Neutrons stabilise the nucleus when they are combined with protons, because they are never rejected: they are always attractive.

There are only ninety-two elements in nature. Why? Why can't you keep on adding protons and neutrons until you have supergiant atoms?

Nuclei are a bit similar to human pyramids. If a group of five or six people get into a circle and hold each other tightly, it will be very difficult for one of them to fall. Even if one of them lost their balance, all the others would hold him or her. They create a structure as solid as the nucleus of chemical elements with few neutrons, such as lithium or chlorine. In them the particles are very closely-knit. The human pyramid becomes more fragile as we add floors to it. There comes a point when, no matter how tightly each person is held onto the others, anyone's slightest movement or slip can destabilise the whole structure. That's what happens in atomic nuclei. When you gather many protons and neutrons, the forces that hold them together become more sensitive to imbalances, which accentuates the repulsion between protons. Nuclei with more than 83 protons are naturally unstable. Uranium has got 92, thorium, 90 and radium, 88.

When a human pyramid collapses, part of the structure stays on the ground and the rest of it falls. In a uranium nucleus, what gets thrown out are not people, but two protons and two neutrons, which form a ball. To make it sound a bit more mysterious, physicists call it the "α particle". The process of nuclear collapse is called "disintegration". Do you want to experience an emission of uranic rays? Get comfortable:

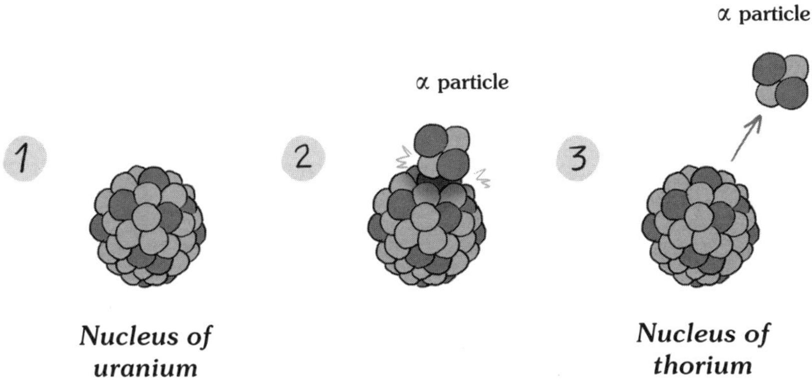

In 1), uranium behaves like the human tower when it is stable. In 2), someone has moved a little, and although the other members of the nucleus fight to retain it, there is an α particle already coming out. In 3) it flies off the nucleus. The result is a smaller tower, with less neutrons and protons: a nucleus of thorium.

Some plants absorb uranium from the ground and, when we eat them, it goes into our bodies. So we too emit uranic rays! However, in our bodies there is hardly 0.1 mg of the element, an irrelevant amount. Only when you put together many atoms of uranium, as it happens in pitchblende, the amount of nuclei that disintegrate produce enough projectiles (alpha particles) for it to be considered radioactive.

A combustion that is not at all spontaneous

Combustions have as their protagonists three chemical elements: oxygen, carbon and hydrogen. Oxygen is in the air and carbon and hydrogen are combined in thousands of ways in fuels, which can be solid, liquid or gas. If you could observe wood, butane gas or petrol with a super magnifying glass, you would find in them a huge amount of atoms of hydrogen and carbon.

In order to see clearly what happens in a combustion, we are going to use one of the simplest types of fuel, methane gas, which is an ingredient of natural gas. Its molecules are formed by one atom of carbon and four of hydrogen. In turn, oxygen molecules contain two atoms of oxygen.

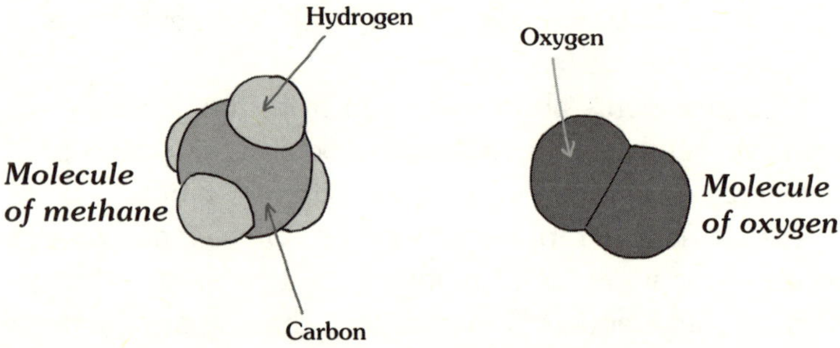

A molecule of methane and a molecule of oxygen, getting ready for a good combustion.

At room temperature, the molecules of methane and oxygen ignore one another, even if they clash against each other. The atoms of hydrogen are holding onto the atoms of carbon very tightly, and they don't feel like letting go of them. The same thing happens with each pair of atoms of oxygen. To begin with, most fuels are quite reluctant to interact with oxygen if it's not very hot. That's a very good thing. Otherwise, with all the carbon, hydrogen and oxygen that there is all around the planet, we would be burning all day long.

For combustion to take place, the molecules need to increase their speed and clash strongly against each other, so that the atoms can become loose and get joined again, forming new molecules. Temperature is nothing but the level of movement of molecules in matter. If the matter is hot, the molecules move very fast; if it is cold, they prefer to stay still.

When a fuel is heated up, its molecules get excited and start to clash against each other increasingly fast. There comes a point when they clash against each other so strongly that they break. Then the atoms become loose and change couples. The carbon and hydrogens of methane gas share the loose atoms of oxygen and form water and carbon dioxide. A combustion has just taken place:

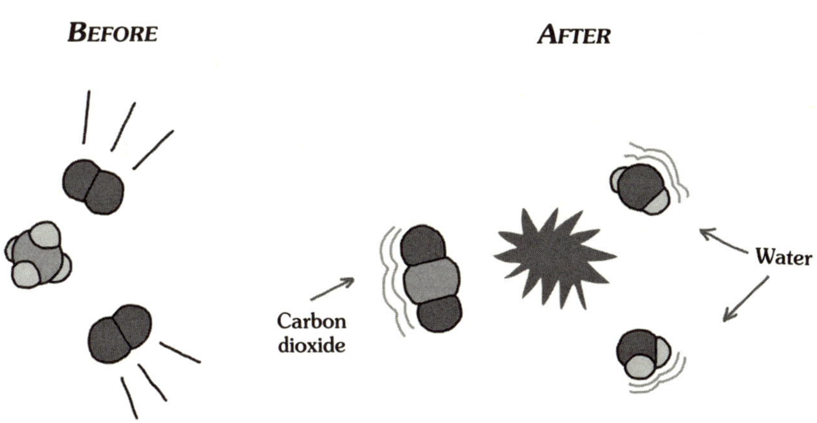

Why does this rearrangement of atoms generate heat? With their recent clash, the molecules of carbon dioxide and water that have just been formed move faster than those of oxygen and methane. They are hotter. As they can't stop still, they clash against other molecules around them and transmit them their excess energy, making them also move faster. This triggers a chain of new combustions. Faster oxygens clash against faster methanes and form more molecules of hot carbon dioxide and water, which in turn clash against other molecules, accelerating them and leading them to combustion. The electrons form the atoms are also affected by the excitement, and in order to relax, they can emit light.

To sum up, fire needs a little push to overcome laziness and get started, but once it does start, it supports itself. The result of each combustion is a certain amount of fast molecules that clash against others, and when they do so they communicate them the necessary speed for them to also react.

That is the reason why a good strategy to put out a fire is to reduce the temperature. If molecules stop, they don't clash strongly enough to break and change couples. When you blow a match, you make the hot gas around the flame move away, and when it becomes cold it stops burning. Water consumes a lot of heat when it evaporates, as you have probably noticed when you sweat, and for that reason, it is ideal for putting out fires.

Explosive living beings

What is gunpowder? That's a good question. It consists of a mixture of charcoal, sulphur and saltpetre. But let's go step by step. Charcoal is composed, almost entirely, of atoms of carbon, with a little bit of hydrogen and a pinch of oxygen. Sulphur is a very common element, and we can find it in minerals or proteins. And what about saltpetre? It is produced by bacteria when they feed from vegetable and animal waste. If we watched it with a magnifying glass powerful enough to distinguish molecules, this is what we would find:

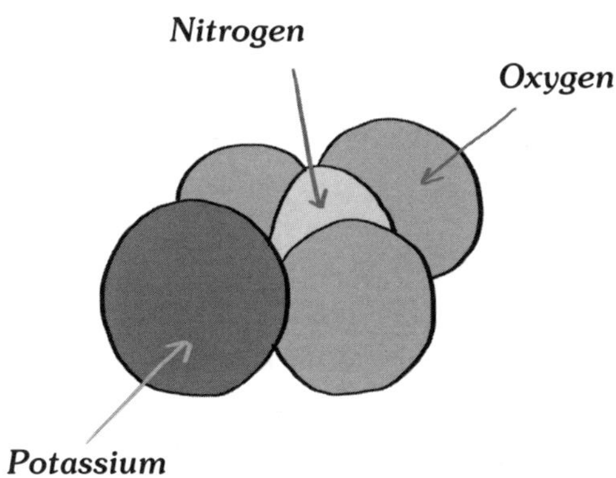

A molecule of saltpetre, with its three oxygens, its nitrogen and its potassium.

What makes this mixture of charcoal, sulphur and saltpetre such an explosive cocktail? Charcoal provides the atoms of carbon that we would expect to find in any combustion. Sulphur has a bit of a secondary role: it reduces the temperature of the reaction and makes it generate less smoke. The key then lies in saltpetre. If you pay attention to the molecule, you will see that it has got a big dose of oxygen. It is like feeding the fire! Besides, it contains nitrogen, an element that is turned into gas at the slightest provocation. Thanks to the sulphur and the oxygen from saltpetre, gunpowder burns very fast. Thanks to the nitrogen, many more gases are generated than in a normal combustion. If gunpowder is put in a confined space, the violent expansion of the gases will cause a big explosion.

It seems funny that the main ingredients of gunpowder (oxygen, nitrogen and carbon) have been produced by living beings. It's something we all suspected. Life is a blast!

OXYGEN

Without it combustion is absolutely impossible. In fact, fire is nothing but a very fast oxidation process, that is, a process in which other elements are combined with oxygen. Most atoms enjoy doing it, so it is no surprise that nearly everything on the surface of the Earth contains some oxygen.

The air around us has also got a huge amount of it: in the atmosphere there are 1 000 000 000 000 000 tonnes in gaseous state. However, the primitive atmosphere of our planet had hardly any oxygen at all. So where did it come from then? About 2 500 million years some very special bacteria started to proliferate. They were capable of producing molecules of oxygen from water, light and carbon dioxide. They soon passed their invention (photosynthesis) to plants and that's how, little by little, the atmosphere became full of oxygen.

NITROGEN

Nitrogen's chemical behaviour couldn't be any more different from that of oxygen. The atom of nitrogen is extremely lazy when it comes to interacting with the other elements. It would gladly spend its entire existence, happily, in a gaseous state, together with another atom of nitrogen. 78% of the air you breathe is nitrogen, but it leaves your nose as easily as it comes in, because it doesn't interact at all.

There are basically three ways to make it come down to the ground. The first one is to hit it with a lightning in a storm, which forces it to combine with oxygen and then drags it onto the ground in rain water. Once on the surface, plants absorb it. There are also some microorganisms that are capable of taking it directly from the air and incorporating it into their cells. Among these, there are some that colonise the roots of legumes. The third way is through industrial processes, which started to be developed from the 19th century onwards.

CARBON

The atoms of carbon show an amazing ability to combine with others to form stable structures, and this is a circumstance that makes carbon atoms the bricks in the construction game of nature. For this reason, many sources of carbon (oil, natural gas or wood) have a biological origin. About 16 kg out of what an average person weighs are carbon, and a great part of what we eat, such as fibre, sugars, fats or proteins are compounds of carbon (we ingest about 300 g a day). Does this make us walking cans of petrol? You may have heard about spontaneous combustion, but don't worry, although 23% of your body is carbon, 65 % is water.

The enemy at home

Your brain

The first lesson at a detective school could be this one: don't trust your senses. And trust even less other people's senses! In the adventure, the young Nemo explains how when a sound is made at the same distance from both ears, the brain hasn't got enough information to know if it is being made in front of it or behind it.

You can try it yourself. Ask a friend to stand in the middle of a room and tell him to close his eyes (without cheating). Explain to him (or her) that you are going to clap your hands many times and that he has to tell you where he is hearing them. Stand in front of him or behind him and each time you clap your hands, make sure that your hands are at the same distance from both his ears. Does he always get it right?

When we see or hear, we don't perceive the light or the sounds as a video camera would. Our brain doesn't use every single piece of information that the senses transmit to

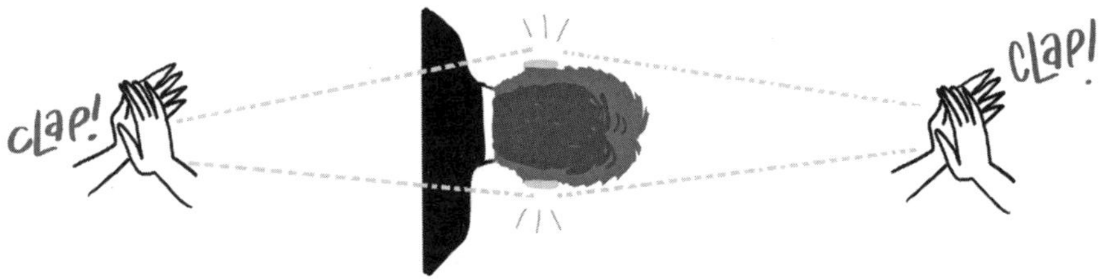

it. It rather uses the information to create a coherent picture of what's happening around you. If it finds any gaps or contradictions, it tries to solve them before telling you what's going on. It also tries to eliminate unnecessary repetitions or details that it doesn't consider interesting enough. What would your perception of the world be like if you received all the information exactly as it comes from your senses? Hold on tight, because this is going to be shaky:

1) You would see everything upside down.

The crystalline lens projects on the retina an inverted image. So new-borns see everything upside down (now it will be easier for you to understand why they sometimes seem to be amazed and why they dribble so much). The brain soon adapts the visual sensations to its experience. Babies learn that when they kneel down they touch the ground and not the sky, or that in order to take the rattle that has been left on the sofa they need to raise their hand and not lower it. There comes a moment when their brain automatically translates all the images it gets and turns them upside down. There have been some experiments made with special glasses that invert the images. A few days after using them, the brain of the people who are wearing them becomes readjusted, and all of a sudden, they can again "see" the world upright.

2) You would be incapable of withdrawing from background noises and loads of superfluous sensations.

You would be hearing all the time the buzz of traffic, the humming of your computer, the rhythm or your breathing, the sound you make when you swallow... You would also constantly feel the pressure of your chair on your back and buttocks, your feet on the ground… Your brain filters out all those impressions, which are not really interesting to you.

3) You would find two holes in your visual field.

They are the blind spots. In your retina there is a small region that has no light-detecting cells, so part of the image that is projected on it is lost. It's as if in the inside of a photographic camera there were some missing detectors to cover a portion of the image. Your retina reserves that space for the optic nerve, which works like a cable that connects your eye to your brain, to transmit to it the images that the crystalline lens projects. In order to prevent you from becoming anxious when you see a whole in the world, the brain "paints" the gap, getting inspiration from the visual information of the immediate surroundings.

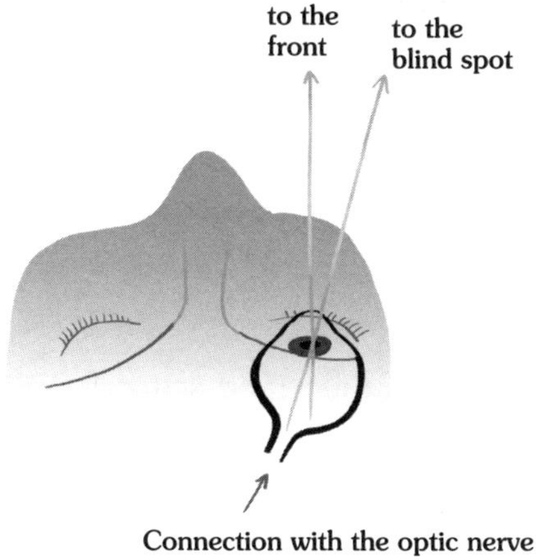

A hole that you don't perceive: the point where the optic nerve is connected to the retina to collect visual information and transmit it to the brain.

You can carry out a simple experiment to unmask your brain's tricks and notice how you really have two blind spots in your eyes. Look at the following picture:

Close your right eye and fix your left eye on Nemo's face. Now, very slowly, take the page of the book closer to you and then further away from you, until Johan's serious face disappears. Where has it gone? The light that comes from that area of the picture is going to your blind spot, and that's why you can't see it.

4) You will have the impression that there is an earthquake around you.

Do you remember any scene from a film that has been shot with the camera on the cameraman's shoulder? The images tremble, jump and seem to be cut while he walks, goes down the stairs, jumps or runs. If you think about it, that's exactly what should happen to your head when you move. However, your brain eliminates all those shakes and offers you an illusion of stability.

5) You would end up exhausted by the hyperactivity of your eyes.

Even when your eyes are still, the movements of the pupil remind of a fly that never stops moving, jumping from one place to another. It can reach thirty-four movements per second! Try the following experiment: when you stop reading spend some time noticing the movement of your eyes, and where you focus them each time. You will notice that you can only see clearly the area around the point on which you are focusing your attention. As if they were pieces from a jigsaw puzzle, your brain gathers all those jumping visual impressions and composes with them a wider virtual image.

After revising the last five points you will agree that your brain works hard in order to make your life easier. It intervenes in your perception in order to avoid a data overload and allows you to concentrate and think without distractions. Studying seems more comfortable when you are not paying attention to the ticking of a clock or walking without the feeling that everything is trembling around you. The main drawback, when it comes to preparing its report, is that the brain can delete important information or fill gaps with perceptions that are not real.

In 1999, Daniel Simons and Christopher Chabris, from Harvard University, carried out one of the most famous experiments in the history of psychology. They played a video to many people. In the video there were three students playing with two basketballs. Three of them were wearing white t-shirts and the other three, black t-shirts. The six of them didn't stop moving and crossing one another, while they passed the ball once and again, always to a player of their same colour. The goal was to count how many passes the players in white made. Easy? The next question that the researchers asked you was if you had seen a gorilla. What gorilla? That's the same question that 46% of the participants in the experiment asked. When they rewinded the video they were amazed to discover that at one point a person dressed up as a gorilla entered the scene, made his way through the six players and then left.

Why hadn't they seen it? Because their brains had filtered it out. They had received instructions to count the number of passes and their attention had been focused on following the players in white. The dark-haired gorilla was perceived as part of the background noise (the players in black), that they shouldn't pay attention to. What's the moral of this story? We very frequently see what we expect to see.

The brain can't stand the absence of sensory stimuli, because its jobs precisely consists in processing them. If your sight, touch, taste or hearing don't offer any information… it invents it. In the 1960s, the first experiments with tanks of sensory deprivation were made. Some volunteers were introduced in hermetically closed chambers, with insulated walls, which didn't let any light or noise come in. Their inside reminded of a bathtub filled with a saline solution, at the same temperature as the skin. When someone was immersed in it, their body floated, in such a way that the feeling of gravity was completely lost. After a few hours in the dark, in absolute silence, without any more perceptions than their own heartbeats, the people inside the tank experienced all sorts of hallucinations. Their brains, bored to death, invented their own impressions so as to have something to do.

Will you dare to...?

Detect the invisible

Each time you breathe out, you let carbon dioxide out. Everybody says so, but how can they be so sure? After all, it's a colourless gas which doesn't smell either. Well, however invisible it is, we are going to see it coming out of your lungs.

The essential ingredient of this experiment has a wonderful name: calcium hydroxide. Its appearance, however, seems quite ordinary: some white powder. Where can you get it? It's usually sold wholesale in shops that sell chemical products, for example, or in department stores of construction materials. It's also used in gardening and aquariums. You can even find it at some chemists. Ask for it in any of these places. As you only need a tea-spoonful, they may even give it to you for free.

In order to see carbon dioxide we are going to need to provoke a very simple chemical reaction. You will probably have the same problem that Marie had at your age: that you won't have a laboratory at hand. A good option could be to ask your teacher to do the experiment in class. If that is not a possibility, we will have to use your home, but there you will have to behave like a real scientist. To begin with, you will need a Pierre Curie to help you, that is, an adult. To manipulate hydroxide, use latex gloves and put on a mask that you can find at any ironmonger's. When it comes to taking precautions, treat as if it were bleach.

Once you have the hydroxide, the rest is easy as pie. You only need a one litre glass bottle, a glass and a straw. Fill the bottle with water and dissolve in it the calcium hydroxide. Stir it well and let it stand for one day. Not all the powder is going to be dissolved, and you need to wait until the remaining powder is deposited at the bottom of the bottle. Close the bottle tightly, and put a label on it so that everyone knows what it has inside, and put it somewhere where it can't be confused with water by mistake.

When the contents of the water show a crystalline appearance, pour about an inch (a finger) of the liquid in a glass. There you have your carbon dioxide detector.

Carbon dioxide caught by surprise.

How does it work? Put the straw in the glass and blow through it, being careful not to suck up. You will see how the liquid undergoes a dramatic metamorphosis! It loses its transparency and acquires a milky colour. To intensify the effect you can blow softly many times.

What has happened? The carbon dioxide has provoked a chemical reaction. The atoms of calcium from the hydroxide have changed their couples and have trapped the carbon dioxide, forming a new molecule: calcium carbonate. This molecule is not soluble and remains suspended in water, giving it a whitish colour.

When you have finished the experiment, throw the liquid from the glass and the bottle in the sink, so that no one mistakes them for water or milk. Let water run for quite some time. Then wash up both the glass and the bottle with plenty of water.